The

UNDERGROUND RAILROAD

in the Adirondack

TOWN *of* CHESTER

The
UNDERGROUND
RAILROAD
in the Adirondack
TOWN *of* CHESTER

DONNA LAGOY *and* LAURA SELDMAN

THE
History
PRESS

Published by The History Press
Charleston, SC
www.historypress.net

Front cover: The Darrowsville Wesleyan Methodist Church with cemetery in 2012. *Courtesy Laura Seldman.* Chain. *Courtesy Mr. S.*

First published 2016

ISBN 978.1.46711.916.0

Library of Congress Control Number: 2016939297

Notice: The information in this book is true and complete to the best of our knowledge. It is offered without guarantee on the part of the authors or The History Press. The authors and The History Press disclaim all liability in connection with the use of this book.

CONTENTS

CONTENTS

ACKNOWLEDGEMENTS

*W*e are grateful to the following people and organizations for their invaluable support and contributions: Sally Baxter, Lynne Bennett, Barbara Davidson, Laura and Wayne Dewey, Marion Eagan, Bob Frye, Amy Godine, Deb Grana, Michael Guarino, Craig Leggett, Cathie Little, Lenore Miller, David Morris, New York Historical Society, Don Papson, Bruce Robbins Sr., Mr. S., LouAnn Springer, Sharon Waddell and Judith Wellman.

Special thanks to the Historical Society of the Town of Chester, which actively supported this Underground Railroad book through its archival resources, financial resources and a network for community involvement. More special thanks to Neil Seldman for his assistance in researching and writing the chapter on the history of the Underground Railroad and to Chloe Seldman for her photographic expertise and for sharing this adventure.

INTRODUCTION

Old Traditions and New Research

The Town of Chester, New York, was an active part of the Underground Railroad (UGRR) northern escape route. With its help, and guided by the North Star,[1] many runaway slaves followed this road to freedom. While most of today's residents have known this through stories about local abolitionists, the issue has never been explored in depth in the town. Some were familiar with the history of the Underground Railroad, since they could trace their ancestors to the Civil War and earlier. Reports of safe houses had been briefly mentioned in articles and books about the Adirondack region, but no oral histories had ever been recorded, and the Museum of Local History had never gathered artifacts, photographs or information relating to the presence of the Underground Railroad in the town. Nor was the town aware that Upstate New York's leading abolitionist, Gerrit Smith, had recognized its citizens as "the truest of men" because of their commitment to the antislavery movement. His revealing journal of his tour of the region, published in the *Albany Patriot* in June 1845, was buried in historical archives.

Our book started with the Darrowsville Wesleyan Methodist Church. The abandoned church was falling apart, posing a serious risk to the community. In 2012 concerned Chester residents met to discuss their collective problem. Although the church was known to be part of the Underground Railroad, and therefore of great historical significance,

Darrowsville Church with sunflowers. *Courtesy Laura Seldman.*

its original owner, the Wesleyan Methodist Connection, declined to take responsibility and would not fund a rebuilding of the structure. After resolving ownership issues, the historical society and town representatives, pressured by the church's imminent total collapse, chose to deconstruct it, preserve some of the original building materials and erect a memorial. This public memorial will tell the story of the hamlet of Darrowsville, including its role in the Underground Railroad.

An architecturally designed memorial, featuring the original church bell and educational storyboards, is under construction (scheduled for completion in the summer of 2016), with strong support from the Historical Society of the Town of Chester, local businesses and local volunteer carpenters. As part of the fundraising for this project, the historical society in 2013 commissioned us—historian Donna Lagoy and photographer Laura Seldman—to create a small documentary photography book entitled *The Darrowsville Church on the Underground Railroad*. In response to this book, and to publicity about the Darrowsville Church, individuals came forward with other stories, some previously unknown, about the Underground Railroad in the Town of Chester. Further, we reached out with flyers and notices in local newsletters and made inquiries in the Town of Chester and neighboring towns.

The board of trustees of the historical society then decided to support a full exploration of the Underground Railroad in the Town of Chester and commissioned us to examine the body of evidence, interview safe house residents, research archives and photograph sites for a comprehensive book.

We therefore undertook the task of documenting Underground Railroad activities in the Town of Chester, turning the town legends into a historical legacy. We literally searched for clues to solve historical mysteries. In order to collect oral histories, we prepared questionnaires and statement release forms and digitally recorded and transcribed narratives. We also reviewed newspapers of the period, viewed vintage photographs, interviewed specialists in the field and researched materials at the Museum of Local History of the Town of Chester, the North Star Underground Railroad Museum, the New York Historical Society and the Library of Congress. We examined Gerrit Smith's account of his 1845 tour of Upstate New York and uncovered another obscure resource, written in 1960, by William Wessels. He reported UGRR activities, citing his sources as specific Adirondack town historians. For each of the eight possible private safe houses, we searched the census, deeds, family letters, town archives and antislavery newspapers and investigated found objects.

Part I of this book, "Looking at History," begins with a brief overview of the Underground Railroad and the abolitionist movement in order to provide a context for understanding the role of the Underground Railroad cluster in the Town of Chester. Chapter 2 gives readers a history of the town and includes details about transportation and the plank road. Chapter 3 presents the Wellman Scale, a guide to rating Underground Railroad sites on their authenticity, and Chapter 4, "Our Beginning," tells the story of two churches. In Part II, "Found," Chapter 5 examines the residential Town of Chester Underground Railroad sites, paired with oral histories. Chapter 6 describes the Town of Chester individuals and clues to connections to the abolitionist movement. Chapter 7 introduces two additional nearby "stations." Chapter 8 presents the objects found at safe house sites that establish the material culture of the period. Chapter 9 discusses the role of archaeology in revealing new information. Finally, the section titled "Looking Backward and Forward" summarizes our observations. Several appendices follow: a timeline, a reprinting of the Warren County portion of Gerrit Smith's tour, an excerpt from memoirs of Abel Brown and a review of estimates of the number of runaway slaves.

Among the new findings of our research are details that confirm the membership of Chester citizens in abolitionist organizations, attest to meetings of local Liberty Party officials and name active town abolitionists not associated with one particular site. We identified two previously unrecognized Underground Railroad stations in neighboring towns, one just south of Chester, in Warrensburg, and one just north, in Schroon Lake. We also confirmed the existence of a cluster of safe houses within the Town of Chester with links to the northern trunk of the New York City–Albany/Troy–Canada UGRR.

This text is enlivened with contemporary color photographs of sites and artifacts. Photographs can explore history with evocative imagery so the viewer can feel present in the remembered past. They reveal the content and context of living history, illuminating the stories that connect the past and the present.

Methodology

Our project documents the activities of the Underground Railroad in the area of the Town of Chester through research from primary and secondary source materials and connects the facts to broader historical issues of slavery and abolition. As historians we seek to find and then put together pieces of the past and to do research and gather information that can help us better understand the Underground Railroad and tell the story in its full context. Our goal is to emulate the work of Underground Railroad historians Wilbur Siebert and William Still in the nineteenth century. The histories they recorded were those of fugitive slaves; the voices we have recorded represent abolitionists. Fugitive voices were not traceable in the Town of Chester.

We encountered a major challenge: we lack consolidated and detailed written records on the activities of the Underground Railroad in Chester and its surroundings. This situation is neither surprising nor accidental. While some benevolent societies, vigilance committees and prominent individuals kept written records of their activities, the majority of people involved in the Underground Railroad were not likely to leave paper trails of their activities or identify their underground contacts. The aiding and abetting of fugitive slaves in the United States during the nineteenth century was, after all, a highly controversial and illegal activity, punishable by fine, branding, incarceration and enslavement. Most of what transpired was never recorded. Researchers must rely on the oral histories handed down through families, property owners and others. Because most fugitives involved in the Underground Railroad were illiterate, and because many families were divided over the issue of slavery, much of the history of the Underground

Town of Chester assessment records show Charles Fowler as assessor and Oliver Arnold as property owner. *Courtesy Laura Seldman.*

Railroad has been forever lost, carried untold to the grave by the brave souls who had been the Underground Railroad.

Two other causes for the paucity of written records are the occurrence of two separate fires in the Town of Chester before 1885 and the lack of local newspapers in the North Country before 1855.[2]

Our research has begun to fill in details in the record. Our methods include locating names and ages in census records, identifying buildings and landowners on contemporary maps, finding the original membership lists of organizations and churches and reading accounts of specific events in old newspapers. Some of our methodological considerations are summarized below.

Oral Tradition

Oral tradition can help fill in the gaps in the largely unwritten history of the Underground Railroad. Stories handed down through generations can contain valuable information on names, dates, locations, events and

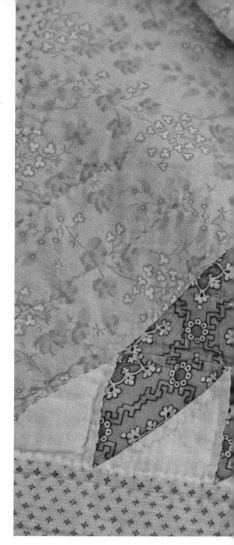

connections that can sometimes lead to archival sources and further research. The purpose of oral history interviews is to create a record that can then be preserved. It is important to ensure that narrators voluntarily give their consent to be interviewed. The interviewer should secure a release form, by which the narrator transfers his or her rights to the interview to the designated individual or organization. Interviewers need to conduct background research on the topic and the larger context in order to ask informed questions.

The interviews provide in-depth accounts of personal experiences and reflections, with sufficient time allowed for the narrators to tell their stories in full. Our narrators were the current owners of the suspected safe house sites. Some were descendants of the houses' original owners; others purchased their property from traceable earlier owners.

To evaluate oral traditions about the Underground Railroad, we used the Wellman Scale, which is based on the reasonableness of the story and the presence or absence of corroborating evidence.[3]

Archaeology and Material Culture

Artifacts found at "station" sites inform us of details of life on the Underground Railroad. In the Town of Chester, current residents found quilts, pottery, a chain and a variety of wood, tin and glass items. Known as material culture, these artifacts are relevant because of the places where they were found: possible safe houses. These historical objects allow us to appreciate the conditions and experiences of both passengers and operators of the UGRR, just as museum exhibits allow us to feel closer to the reality of previous eras. For example, hand-carved wooden shoe forms were found at two of the nine sites. The fugitives' need for shoes was a known part of the

Quilt experts pointed out that two different quilts owned by the Leggetts utilized the same fabrics and were probably sewn by the same hand. *Courtesy Laura Seldman.*

UGRR story. It was surprising to see nine different hand-pieced quilts at safe house sites. These quilts had to be carefully analyzed for age and materials by textile professionals. Scholars now agree that quilts were absolutely not part of a secret code or messages on the Underground Railroad.

Artifacts and building remains unearthed by archaeologists can make a rich contribution to the understanding of the past. In the Town of Chester, only one possible safe house site has been professionally excavated.

Undoubtedly there is more to be discovered at these now recorded sites.

Part I
LOOKING AT HISTORY

1.

BRIEF HISTORY OF THE
UNDERGROUND RAILROAD

*B*etween 1525 and 1866 nearly 390,000 Africans were transported directly to the United States for the slave trade, in a journey known as the Middle Passage. Although the U.S. Constitution forbade the importation of slaves after 1808, illegal smuggling continued. Perhaps as many as 70,000 more ended up in the United States from the more than 10 million African slaves who were shipped to the Caribbean and South America.[4] They were primarily brought to support the economy of the South in the labor-intensive production of crops such as sugar, coffee, cacao, tobacco and rice.

When Eli Whitney invented and patented the cotton gin in 1794, it prompted an immediate explosive growth in the cotton industry and the need for many more hands for picking in the fields. "King Cotton" changed the American landscape. The yield of raw cotton doubled each decade. The gin made it possible to supply large quantities of cotton fiber to the fast-growing textile industry in New England. Britain, the most powerful nation in the world, relied on slave-produced American cotton for over 80 percent of its essential industrial raw material.[5] Within ten years, the value of the U.S. cotton crop rose from $150,000 to more than $8 million.[6]

So began the Second Middle Passage, during which approximately one million enslaved people were relocated from the upper South to the lower South, mostly through the domestic slave trade.[7] This expanded labor force and the constant depletion of soil drove southern planters to increase their territories for new plantations. For this purpose, in an act of unscrupulous acquisitiveness, Native Americans were forcibly removed from their land following the Louisiana Purchase (known as the Trail of Tears in 1838).

The dreadful tragedy of enslaved workers forced to labor under violent tactics of owners or overseers, sexual cruelties and deliberate separation of families has been recorded in thousands of slave histories gathered by Still, Siebert and the Federal Writers' Project.[8] In addition, a genre of literature called Slave Narratives (204 separately published autobiographical texts) offers vivid first-person accounts, with gruesome details about brutal slave life on a southern plantation.

The Underground Railroad was an instrument for radical social change that galvanized thousands of Americans to help an estimated 30,000 to 150,000 runaway slaves make their way to freedom. Runaways were just a tiny proportion of the estimated four million slaves held in the United States in 1860, less than one half of 1 percent.[9] Yet their efforts to escape severely undercut the argument that slavery was a benign, morally sound institution. The Underground Railroad fanned the simmering flames of resentment from slave owners that led to the violent end of slavery in the Civil War.

The phenomenon of runaway slaves is as old as the institution of slavery. Slaves in America fled their masters at every opportunity for generations: south to Florida, west to Indian lands, southwest to Mexico and north to more compassionate states en route to Canada, where Britain had banned slavery since 1833. "If proximity to free territory prompted slaves to run away, so, too did living near areas where runaways congregated 'outlaw' camps...deep in the woods or swamps."[10]

"No matter how diligent, punitive or lenient: no matter how imaginative, ingenious or attentive: no matter how determined, compassionate, or brutal, they [slave owners] remained unable to halt the stream of slaves that left plantations and farms."[11] The Revolutionary War provided a great opportunity for flight, since British governors promised freedom to slaves who joined their side. Thousands ran away in 1775, when Lord Dunmore, the royal governor of Virginia, proclaimed "Liberty for Slaves" who aided the British. Historian Simon Schama considers the immediate "emancipation of tens of thousands of slaves" an "astounding" result of Dumore's declaration. The British generals Howe and Clinton extended the definition of those entitled to liberty to black women and children.[12]

Even before the 1800s, a system to abet runaways seems to have existed. George Washington complained in 1786 that one of his runaway slaves was aided by "a society of Quakers, formed for such purposes." Quakers had developed systematic methods for passing escapees to safety, including passwords, secret abodes and clandestine travel. Quakers, more correctly called the Religious Society of Friends, were among the earliest abolition groups. Their influence may have been part of the reason Pennsylvania, where many Quakers lived, was the first state to ban slavery.[13]

The name "Underground Railroad" may have had several origins. One legend has it that Tice Davids, a Kentucky slave escaping his pursuers, swam across the Ohio River and immediately disappeared, probably meeting up with an abolitionist "agent" in Ripley, Ohio. "The angry slave owner was heard to say, 'He must have gone off on the underground railroad.'"[14] Eric Foner refers to an 1839 newspaper article quoting a runaway slave who "hoped to escape on a railroad that 'went underground all the way to Boston.'"[15]

By the 1830s, the many spontaneous individual efforts to house, clothe, feed and acclimate fugitives had coalesced into an informal, loosely organized network. As actual iron-and-steel railroads became increasingly familiar sights throughout the states, the concept of a parallel "underground railroad" that moved people on regular schedules captured the popular imagination. This form of transport, though, was clandestine and carried its passengers without rails or steam. The Underground Railroad used many of the same terms as a regular railroad: "agents" directed fugitives to safe "stations" or "depots," "conductors" guided travelers to the next station some five to ten miles away and "stockholders" or "investors" raised money for court hearings and lobbying.

Operators on the Underground Railroad moved passengers, referred to as "Southern goods," secretly, utilizing railroads, wagons, ships and horses or by guided treks on foot. Free blacks and successful runaways, men and women, members of the business elite and common workers, ship captains, railroad workers, the educated and the illiterate coordinated transportation, food and clothing and arranged for jobs and farms for fugitives transplanted from slavery. All joined what David Ruggles, a leading black abolitionist, declared to be the day-to-day work of "practical abolitionism" in the great effort for humanity.[16]

On its website "Exploring a Common Past: Researching and Interpreting the Underground Railroad," the National Park Service states that historians may have overestimated the abolitionists' role in the Underground Railroad: "[T]he majority of assistance to runaways came from slaves and free blacks and the greatest responsibility for providing shelter, financial support and direction to successful runaways came from the organized efforts of northern free blacks."[17] To this Henry Louis Gates

Jr. added the words, "and sympathetic whites" in his documentary *African Americans: Many Rivers to Cross.*[18]

Women as well as men fed, clothed, nursed, hid and escorted escapees to safe houses on their journey north. While sometimes women led groups of runaway slaves, at other times they provided support and backup, assisting anonymously.

The Underground Railroad consisted of an extensive network stretching from the southern slave states all the way north to freedom across the Canadian border. Most runaways came from states bordering free northern and western states. "The Underground Railroad was at their very door," Virginia's governor, Henry Wise, lamented. He said that in the mid-1850s in his borderland state, "slaves can liberate themselves by running away."[19] In New York, fugitives arrived at the major depots in Albany and Troy from New York City and then traveled either west through Syracuse, Rochester and Ohio to reach free black communities in Ontario, Canada, or due north up the Hudson River toward the Champlain Valley and Adirondack Mountains en route to Montreal or eastern Canada.

After the 1850 passage of the second Fugitive Slave Act, which required that U.S. citizens anywhere assist in the apprehension of runaways, Canada became the main safe haven for freedom seekers, remaining so through the end of the Civil War. Still, not all former slaves immigrated to Canada. There are accounts of some, like John Thomas, who chose to settle in the communities of the Adirondacks. It is rumored that slave catchers located Thomas at his home near Franklin Falls, but when they came to capture him, they were told that local whites would defend Thomas if a confrontation arose. The slave catchers chose to give up.[20]

The Fugitive Slave Clause in the U.S. Constitution of 1789 and the first Fugitive Slave Law of 1793 did not require governments to participate actively in capturing and sending back fleeing slaves to their owners. Before 1850, slave owners, not state or federal governments, were responsible for the recapture of their own property.

New York, New England, Ohio, Michigan and Wisconsin protected runaways by enacting new personal liberty laws that authorized the state to provide counsel for accused fugitives, required jury trials to determine their status and increased penalties for kidnapping free blacks.

The 1850 Fugitive Slave Act gave federal support to southerners who came north to take possession of their escaped chattel and ended any legal rights fugitive slaves might have had under state law. Testimony from accused runaways was prohibited. The fines for harboring runaways were increased

OPERATORS ON THE UNDERGROUND RAILROAD

Perhaps the most remarkable female conductor on the Underground Railroad was **Harriet Tubman**, referred to variously as Moses, a contemporary Joan of Arc, "Queen of the Underground" and the "greatest heroine of the age." She rescued some seventy slaves in thirteen expeditions to the eastern shore of Maryland. A fugitive slave herself, Tubman was helped along the Underground Railroad by another famous conductor, William Still. He went on to write a book, *The Underground Railroad: A Record of Facts, Authentic Narratives, Letters*, that contains descriptions of fugitive slaves' escape to freedom.

Laura Haviland (1808–1898) was regarded as the "Superintendent of the Underground Railroad." In *A Woman's Life Work: Labor and Experiences of Laura S Haviland* (1882), she documented her work as one of the foremost conductors of the Underground Railroad in Michigan, an educator of freed blacks in Canada and a volunteer nurse to wounded Union soldiers in captivity during the Civil War.

Frederick Douglass (1817–1895), born into slavery in the Chesapeake region of Maryland, was taught to read by his master's wife, Lucretia Auld. "Once you learn to read you will be forever free," he wrote in his 1845 autobiography, *Narrative of the Life of Frederick Douglass, an American Slave*. He escaped slavery with the help of David Ruggles and the New York City Underground Railroad. In 1841, he dedicated his life to ending slavery in the United States. His physical presence and charismatic personality soon made him a leading spokesperson and intellectual leader of the abolitionist movement both in the United States and abroad. Douglass published the *North Star* newspaper and served as a conductor on the Underground Railroad in Rochester, New York.

Henry Bibb (1815–1854) escaped from slavery and was recaptured no fewer than five times before he finally succeeded, suffering physical hardship and the loss of his wife and family members, who were sold to new masters. He reached the Underground Railroad in Detroit and became a skilled orator for the abolitionist cause. His autobiography, *Narrative of the Life and Adventures of an American Slave, Written by Himself*, was published in 1849. He worked closely with Mary Ann Shadd on the *Provincial Freeman*.

Dr. Hiram Corliss (1793–1877) was the Underground Railroad stationmaster in Washington County, New York. Legend claims that the doctor had a small, windowless cellar room from which a tunnel led to the banks of the Battenkill River. In 1837 he led the Free Congregational Church (a "comeouter" antislavery church) in Union Village. Comeouter churches were founded by tens of thousands of religious abolitionists based on uncompromised antislavery principles. Most important among them was the Wesleyan Methodist Connection.[21]

Levi Coffin (1798–1877), a leader of the Railroad (and its reputed president), claimed to have helped an average of 100 slaves in his home in Cincinnati every year for thirty-three years.

from $500 to $1,000 for each fugitive. Prison terms for aiding runaways were set at six months for each fugitive. The year 1851 saw the largest number of successful attempts to recapture runaways. Frederick Douglass called the 1850 statute "the odious Bloodhound Law."[22] The new law even encouraged slave owners and their agents to reach far into the Adirondacks. Slavers took revenge on people who were helping runaways by attacking abolitionists in the streets and burning down their homes, meeting places and offices.

Captured fugitive slaves could be flogged, branded, jailed, sold back into slavery or even killed. And since slaves were property, freeing slaves was viewed as stealing. If a conductor was caught helping slaves escape, he or she could be fined, imprisoned, branded or even hanged.

Antislavery sentiment in non-slave states rose to new heights. Northerners realized that there was no place in the country where slavery was against the law. In September 1851, within months of the passage of the Fugitive Slave Act, an attempt to recapture runaways touched off an antislavery riot in Christiana, Pennsylvania, creating a national sensation. Frederick Douglass called the event the "Battle for Liberty." A Pennsylvania newspaper ran the headline "Civil War: First Blow Struck." The Christiana Resistance succeeded in protecting four slaves fleeing their owner and hired slave catchers. The slaves had headed from Maryland to the home of William Parker, a free black man in the Christiana area known for his leadership of the Committee for Mutual Protection. One hundred free blacks and white townspeople, teachers, lawyers, preachers and farmers defended the runaways. The slave owner trying to get his property back was killed in the melee.

At trial, all thirty-eight defendants were acquitted. The fugitives made it to freedom in Canada. "Southerners," wrote one historian, "were stunned at the audacity of Blacks fighting for their own freedom" and were further angered by the support of white people apparently undeterred by the harsh law so recently passed. Southern hopes that henceforth slave owners could recover their human property without obstruction were crushed, as the new law was seen as unenforceable. But abolitionists saw in the Christiana Resistance a righteous "uprising of the oppressed."[23]

The Abolitionist Movement

The Underground Railroad drew strength from the abolitionist movement, which worked on many fronts to end slavery. Quakers had established antislavery societies by 1815, but the abolitionist movement did not become important nationally until 1831, when William Lloyd Garrison founded the Boston-based newspaper the *Liberator*. Garrison made his intentions explicit in his first edition: "In defending the great cause of human rights, I wish to derive the assistance of all religions and of all parties....I shall strenuously contend for the immediate enfranchisement of our slave population." The *Liberator*'s masthead declared, "Our Country is the World; Our Countrymen are all Mankind." In 1834 three-fourths of subscribers were African Americans.[24]

In its work of making a strong moral appeal for abolition, the *Liberator* was joined by more than sixty national newspapers—prominent among them the *North Star*, *Tocsin of Liberty*, *Emancipator*, *National Anti-Slavery Standard* and *Albany Patriot*. Publishers, editors and journalists strove to turn the hearts and minds of Americans, North and South, against the South's "peculiar institution." Public lectures were another important way of spreading the message; speakers were trained and sent on tours. Abolitionists also attended to the needs of runaway slaves, working in various capacities on the Underground Railroad and tutoring fugitives on proper demeanor in a free society.

The abolitionist movement grew and reflected the combined grass-roots fervor of the new religious and temperance movements of the era. The ethical and moral tenets of the movements were deeply connected. The *Albany Patriot*, a Liberty Party newspaper, featured columns on temperance next to ones on abolitionism. The Protestant reform, referred to as "burned over districts," was strong in Upstate and Western New York, pulling many congregations into the abolitionist movement. Breakaway churches were common. These churches, as well as Presbyterians, Evangelical Protestants and Quaker Meetings, formed the religious backbone of the movement.

The *Liberator* also encouraged and publicized the participation of women in the abolitionist movement. In 1832, it launched a weekly column entitled "Ladies Department." And the *Albany Patriot*, an abolitionist newspaper in New York State, published a notice in November 1844 urging women to participate in antislavery activities.

Among other activities, abolitionist women organized annual antislavery fairs (also called bazaars), which started in Boston in 1833 and later spread to many other cities. Through these bazaars, the women raised money to sustain organizations, newspapers or paid staff; in some cases, they passed the money on to help freed or escaping slaves buy clothing, food and riverboat and railroad tickets. "Handsome and tasteful" articles attracted the general public in addition to promoting those eager to support the abolitionist cause.[25]

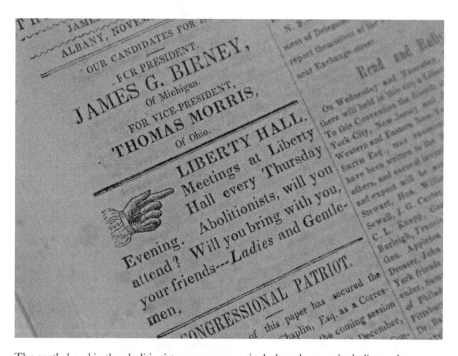

The gentle hand in the abolitionist newspaper particularly welcomes the ladies to the regular meeting. *Courtesy Laura Seldman.*

The *Liberator* described one 1836 fair as follows:

> *The Hall was filled with visitors at an early hour, and continued full until late in the evening. Very many of these were not abolitionists, but belonged to a large and increasing class of the community, who have been strongly abolitionized by Anti-Slavery efforts....The cake table was loaded with varieties of cake, made of sugar not manufactured by slaves, and near it was placed the motto, "Free Labor."*[26]

For nearly twenty years, the *Liberty Bell*, an annual antislavery gift book, was sold at the Boston Bazaar as part of the fundraising effort. The gift book had contributions from notable figures: Henry Wadsworth Longfellow, Ralph Waldo Emerson and Elizabeth Barrett Browning, among others. None of the contributors was paid for his or her contributions aside from receiving a copy of the *Liberty Bell*.

Many traditional quilting bees and sewing circles integrated an antislavery message into their activities. While making articles to sell at antislavery fairs, women were also learning to articulate their beliefs among like-minded women. Charlotte Forten, a young free black woman, wrote on December 6, 1854, "Studied arithmetic and philosophy and in the afternoon went to a sewing party or 'bee' as the New Englanders call it. Such parties possess not the slightest attraction for me, unless they are for the anti-slavery fair. Then I always feel it both a duty and pleasure to go."[27]

TOKEN

In 1837, the *Emancipator*, the weekly newspaper of the American Anti-Slavery Society, advertised a token (a copper coin) bearing a powerful image of a black woman kneeling in chains, saying, "Am I not a woman and a sister?" The appearance of the female icon symbolized a growing awareness of the special hardships that women suffered under slavery as victims of sexual exploitation and also recognized the prominent role that women were playing in the antislavery movement. However, the director of the U.S. Mint quickly suppressed the circulation of the token.

The image was a familiar one to Americans involved in the struggle to end slavery. A similar version, designed and produced by Josiah Wedgwood, featured a male slave and posed the question, "Am I

The image of the abolitionist coin was first shown in the newspaper the *Emancipator*. This photograph is from an exhibit at the New-York Historical Society in 2015. *Courtesy Laura Seldman.*

not a man and a brother?" Wedgwood's medallion appeared in the late 1780s and quickly became an emblem of both the British and American abolitionist causes. Soon afterward, Americans encountered the image everywhere: on porcelain cameos and coins, in newspapers and the title pages of books, on commercial crockery and women's needlework.

These tokens have traditionally been regarded as appealing to a shared humanity. More recently, however, some have viewed the coin image as derogatory: the slave appears to be helpless and begging rather than actively resisting oppression.

In addition to creating articles for sale, sewing circles had the practical application of providing new clothes for fugitives. Slaves typically dressed in easily recognizable "Negro summer cloth" made with checked patterns or homespun stripes. In order to blend in with the rest of society, fleeing blacks needed suitable clothing, including bonnets, gloves and shoes.

But women's antislavery activities were not limited to producing items for bazaars and clothing for runaway slaves. Black and white women served as antislavery lecturers, editors, fundraisers and organizers. Slaveholders fumed at women's activism. The *Southern Literary Messenger* referred to abolitionist women as "politicians in petticoats" who needlessly stirred up trouble on the slavery issue.[28]

Sojourner Truth's lectures were particularly persuasive. Though uneducated and illiterate, she was eloquent and incisive, but because she had been a slave, she provided personal testimony to the horrors of slavery.[29]

Many abolitionist women also advocated related causes, such as equality for women. For instance, the outspoken Quaker sisters Angelina and Sarah Grimke questioned both the legitimacy of the southern slave system and the concept of a proper women's sphere. They challenged the idea of appropriate women's behavior and questioned their own "subordinate" status. As abolitionists, they were committed not only to freeing the enslaved but also to ending racial discrimination and achieving true social and political equality in the United States.

Many participants at the First Women's Rights convention at Seneca Falls, New York, in 1848, including Frederick Douglass and Lucretia and James Mott, were seasoned abolitionists who borrowed phrases and ideas from the antislavery movement in their advocacy of women's rights.

In 1853 Garrison wrote, "I have been derisively called a 'Woman's Rights Man.' I know no such distinction. I claim to be a HUMAN RIGHTS Man."

However, the abolitionist movement was rife with often-bitter differences and ad hominem attacks. There were many different answers to the question, "What is to be done?" Should former slaves be colonized to Africa?

WOMEN ABOLITIONISTS

Underground Railroad researcher Andrea Korgan, author of *Heroes in Petticoats*, has noted the differing roles of numerous female heroines, for the most part unrecognized.[30]

Frances Ellen Watkins Harper was one of the "single most important black woman leaders to figure in both the abolitionist and feminist reform movements," yet she is still practically unknown today. Harper, an educated orator and lecturer, was "sensitive to issues of race, class, and gender."[31]

Lydia Maria Child (1802–1880) was a popular writer recruited to the abolitionist cause by William Lloyd Garrison. In 1833 Child produced *An Appeal in Favor of that Class of Americans Called Africans*, a sensational antislavery statement that won converts to the movement. From 1841 to 1849, she edited the New York–based newspaper *National Anti-Slavery Standard*. Child, one of the original organizers of the Boston antislavery fair, wrote in a letter, "You have doubtless learned the success of our Fair....My cradle-quilt sold for $5." Remarkably, Child's quilt has survived. The Historic New England museum, formerly the Society for the Preservation of New England Antiquities, owns a small star quilt with the exact poem she had inscribed, "Remember the Slave."[32]

In 1835 **Maria Weston Chapman** (1806–1885) assumed the leadership of the Boston Anti-Slavery Bazaar, which had been founded the previous year by Lydia Maria Child and Louisa Loring. Chapman directed the fair until 1858. She and her husband, Henry, were both "Garrisonian" abolitionists; they believed in advocating an immediate rather than a gradual end to slavery, to be achieved by nonresistance and "moral suasion." Chapman, a prolific writer, published *Right and Wrong in Massachusetts* in 1839 and *How Can I Help to Abolish Slavery?* in 1855.

Mary Ann Shadd (Cary) (1823–1893), a free-born African American from Michigan, was a leading abolitionist in the United States and Canada. She was the first woman in North America to edit a newspaper, the *Provincial Freeman*, which encouraged fugitive slaves and free blacks to immigrate to Canada. She developed educational programs for these communities. Frederick Douglass said there was no woman like her in the nation. After the Civil War, Shadd became active in the women's suffrage movement.

Colonizers favored freeing slaves by resettling them in Africa. By 1867 more than thirteen thousand emigrants had been sent to Liberia.[33]

Should the goal be just to free the slaves or to give them complete civil rights? "Amalgamators" argued for complete civil rights, intermarriage and social standing for blacks. Should political tactics be used, as in England, or should the abolitionist movement rely on moral suasion? Some even argued that the Underground Railroad actually delayed the ultimate end of slavery by wasting time and money on individual runaways.

Followers of the Boston abolitionist William Lloyd Garrison viewed the Constitution as a proslavery document that needed to be changed, through public appeals based on morality, with a new concept for emancipation. On the other hand, the philanthropists and manufacturers Arthur and Lewis Tappan and Quaker Isaac Hopper led differently oriented antislavery organizations, espousing political and religious approaches to antislavery activism that the Garrisonians disdained. Yet despite significant differences, as Eric Foner points out, most abolitionists on both sides of the internal debates shared a resolve to assist runaway slaves, a resolve that strengthened after the passage of the Fugitive Slave Act of 1850.

Competition among abolitionist organizations for funding was fierce, including the American Anti-Slavery Society (Garrison), the New York State Antislavery Society (Gerrit Smith), New York City and Albany Vigilance committees, the American Colonization Society, the Boston Female Fair Antislavery Society and the American and Foreign Antislavery Society. By 1837 Massachusetts had 145 antislavery societies, New York had 274 and Ohio had 213.[34]

Fugitives and Slave Catchers in New York City: Melting Pot and Boiling Pot

New York was the most significant slaveholding state north of the Mason-Dixon line. In 1790, nearly 40 percent of the households in the New York City area held slaves—a greater percentage than in any southern state.[35] The number of enslaved people in that area, in that year, was twenty-one thousand, more than in any other northern state. By the 1830s, New York City's slave market was second in size only to that of Charleston, South Carolina. As early as 1785—almost fifty years before the American Anti-Slavery Society was founded in 1833—New Yorkers formed the first Manumission Society to provide legal assistance to runaways. The New York Manumission Society led the lobbying for gradual emancipation. Its efforts paid off in 1817, when the state passed a state law abolishing slavery as of July 4, 1827.

New York City was the epicenter of northern support for the southern cause. Commercial interests intimately linked the banking, railroad and cotton manufacturers in the city with southern planters. Family ties and frequent business trips to and from the South solidified cultural and social affinities. Fergus Bordewich writes in his classic history of the Underground Railroad, *Bound for Canaan*, "New York's prosperity was wedded to the South. The city formed the hinge of the so-called Cotton Triangle....Racism was virulent....The city's political culture was also friendly to slavery....The city was estimated to have 5,000 runaway slaves. An informal and shifting ring was known as the New York Kidnapping Club."[36] Unfortunately, free blacks as well as runaway slaves were the victims of kidnapping.

At the same time, New York City, as the commercial center of the nation, with extensive railroads and shipping lanes, emerged as the critical transportation hub for helping fugitives pass to Albany or Troy in Upstate New York and from there due north to Canada or west to Syracuse and Rochester and through Ohio to established free black communities in Ontario, Canada. As early as the 1820s, southern newspapers complained bitterly that the "increase of Negroes in this place" made New York City "the point of refuge for all runaways in the Union."[37] New York's press was split on the issue of fugitive slaves. The *New York Times* opposed the Fugitive Slave Act of 1850 but maintained that New York should adhere to the law. The *New York Herald*, on the other hand, made no bones about where its sentiments lay, calling the Underground Railroad "fanatical warfare on the constitutional rights of property."[38]

New York City developed the first antislavery societies that protected runaway slaves from recapture and sped them northward to freedom. These associations, as Eric Foner points out, were the first major interracial organizations in the country.[39] They also formed the first civil rights movement in the United States, paralleling the contemporary Chartist movement in England. Slave catchers and bounty hunters roamed New York's streets, searching for runaways on ships, railroad cars and docks. Members of the Underground Railroad roamed the same streets, trying to find fugitives and lead them to safety.

A rash of kidnappings in the city led to the formation of Vigilance Committees, which, relying on city and state laws that required court proceedings before anyone could be re-enslaved, orchestrated large demonstrations at courts, railways and shipyards to prevent the transport of fugitives and captured freemen to the Deep South. Members of these committees also moved people out of danger through the Underground Railroad.

Given its large population of free black people, its extensive water frontage and a warren of city streets that made it difficult for bounty hunters to track fugitives, Brooklyn was a major hub of the Underground Railroad. Antislavery sermons at the Plymouth Congregational Church by its minister, Henry Ward Beecher,[40] were well attended. Because of the large number of freedom seekers who passed through his church, it became known as the Grand Central Depot of the UGRR in New York.[41] Beecher's mock slave auctions, at which he appealed for funds to buy the freedom of actual slaves, attracted even more attention. In 1860 Beecher introduced a new

A MATURE UGRR SERVING THE EAST COAST

Strategies and tactics developed in New York City—finding runaways on the streets, on the docks and hidden in ships and railway cars, conducting them to safe houses, provisioning them and quickly sending them north of the city—were shared with other major cities along the metropolitan corridors of the East Coast, extending feeder lines to Wilmington, Baltimore and Philadelphia. These lines routinely served individuals and groups, some more dramatically than others. In 1849 **Henry "Box" Brown** arrived in Philadelphia by railcar in a box no longer than three feet. By 1850, when Harriet Tubman made her first foray back into slave territory to retrieve her family and others from Maryland, the underground system was fully mature and ready to receive these passengers.

tactic, appealing for funds to buy a nine-year-old child from the auction blocks. The effort succeeded. The goal of these tactics was to arouse a "panic of sympathy." Death threats ensued. But attendance was steady as Beecher invited the cultural stars of the day to speak, including Sojourner Truth, Mark Twain, Charles Dickens and Frederick Douglass. Dickens took three nights to read *A Christmas Carol* to capacity crowds.[42]

Two key players in the Underground Railroad in New York City were Sydney Howard Gay, a well-educated scion of a wealthy New England family, and Louis Napoleon, an illiterate former slave. These consummate conductors on the Underground Railroad engineered thousands of successful escapes. Their *Record of Fugitives*, which was recently discovered, provides the best data on the movements, costs and networks of the working Underground Railroad. This ledger forms the basis of contemporary research on the New York City–Albany/Troy line of the Underground Railroad.[43]

New York's abolitionists belonged to different branches of the movement. Some were Garrisonians. In 1835, they established the New York Committee of Vigilance, which became the center for the city's branch of the Underground Railroad. Others shared the political action approach of the Tappan brothers. But in the face of imminent danger, the oft-quarrelsome abolitionist societies in New York City banded together to maintain the increasingly well-traveled freedom road to the north. In the 1850s, they aided more than one thousand fugitives who arrived in the city.

North of New York City

Fugitives who fled as far as sixty miles north of the city (i.e., to Dutchess County) and their agents could rest more easily. Here the fugitives were "far enough on the way to Canada to find their way safely."[44]

Farther on, in the wilderness of the North Country, fugitives could travel by day and in the open. The population this far from New York City was generally supportive. In one documented case in Keeseville, New York, a farmer found a fugitive sleeping in his barn. He brought out the poster offering a $500 reward for anyone who assisted in the recapture of the fugitive. The farmer fed the runaway and sent him on his way.[45]

However, despite a generally favorable political culture in New York State, danger always lurked. Solomon Northup, a free black living in Saratoga, New York, was lured to Washington, D.C., on the promise of work as a fiddler by two undercover slave catchers. He was kidnapped and enslaved under harsh conditions as described in his 1853 memoir, *Twelve Years a Slave*.

In Glens Falls, in 1851, John Van Pelt, a free black whose neighbors declared him to be "upright and inoffensive," was forced to flee after he married an escaped slave. Alert neighboring youngsters sent the slave catchers to the wrong address, giving the Van Pelts time to escape along old Adirondack military roads to Prescott, Canada.

In the early 1840s, abolitionists from Upstate New York established the Liberty Party. The party offered a vehicle of protest against slavery for those committed to electoral politics. From its earliest days, it struggled with its identity. "Was the party a means of registering a moral protest to slavery or was it a means of gaining power to effect political change?"[46] At the state and local levels, the party had some strength. Some wanted to expand issues beyond slavery. But the national party remained structurally weak throughout its existence. Historians consider the Liberty Party an early antecedent of the Republican Party (founded in 1854), which was able to win political power with the election of Abraham Lincoln in 1860.

VOICE OF THE LIBERTY PARTY

Gerrit Smith, a founder and leader of the Liberty Party, used his inheritance from his father, a partner in the John Jacob Astor fur-trading empire, to buy and cede 120,000 acres of Adirondack farmland to five hundred free blacks and runaway slaves. The small surviving community was called Timbuctoo. Smith also played a role on the national level. He was a member of the Secret Six committee, which funneled money to support John Brown's antislavery raids in Kansas and eventually Brown's assault on Harper's Ferry, West Virginia.

Smith was nominated as an antislavery presidential candidate four times.

Continuing North

Switala's Eastern Route map shows the lines of the Underground Railroad in New York and underscores the critical strategic positions of Albany and neighboring Troy. Arrows represent a loose network of safe houses, a web of alternatives to confuse slavecatchers. Runaways could arrive by rail, wagon,

JOHN BROWN

John Brown, prominent radical abolitionist, settled in Hudson, Ohio, in 1836 and was a busy stationmaster in the Ohio branch of the Underground Railroad. He constructed a hiding place for fugitives in his barn and made regular nighttime trips to transport blacks to stations farther north.

He moved his family to a farm in North Elba, near Lake Placid, in the Adirondacks in 1849 to participate in a new chapter of the Underground Railroad: helping five hundred free blacks and fugitive slaves and their families settle on the 120,000 acres of land that Gerrit Smith had given them to own and operate. Brown hoped to teach farm skills to these new rural residents. The community, known as Timbuctoo, ultimately did not survive the harsh climate, barren land and isolated economy. Brown worked in the Adirondacks from 1849 to 1855. Switala reports that Brown operated an Underground Railroad station in his farm in North Elba, New York.[47] Wessels also writes that Brown served as a stationmaster and conductor on the UGRR there and that Timbuctoo was also a "station."[48]

In 1855–56, "Bleeding Kansas," the unofficial war between pro- and antislavery forces, drew his attention. Brown and five sons moved to the Kansas Territory in October 1855 to support the Free State settlers against the proslavery Missouri Border Ruffians, whose violent attacks and rigged elections put Free State supporters in grave danger.

In May 1856, eight hundred to one thousand armed invaders from Missouri raided Lawrence, Kansas. The town's two newspapers were destroyed, the main hotel was burned and the homes of civic leaders were systematically looted and burned. The townspeople offered no resistance.

Brown thought that by capturing and executing five leaders of the proslavery community, he could teach Free Staters how to defend themselves. Violent battles continued until late 1856, when the new territorial governor negotiated a ceasefire. Scattered violence continued. The experience convinced Brown that slavery could be defeated only by arming blacks and sympathetic white citizens. Brown started preparations for the armed assault on the Federal Armory in Harper's Ferry, West Virginia, with the goal of liberating slaves, arming them to engage in the war for freedom. The conspiracy had the moral and monetary support of wealthy New England abolitionists. "Bleeding Kansas" was the warmup to the Civil War; Harper's Ferry was the spark.

foot and boat. Many headed due west to Syracuse and Rochester or Cincinnati on the way to existing free black communities in Ontario. The nation's first railway suspension bridge in Niagara, New York, was completed in 1855 and aided the escape of runaway slaves to western destinations in Canada. From Albany-Troy, fugitives could continue due north on the Adirondack or Vermont lines of the Underground Railroad. The Champlain Canal, completed in 1823, provided a water passage due north to Canada.

The northern route from Albany was aided by the presence of Quaker individuals and communities in the Capital Region in the 1830s, '40s and '50s, which had established safe houses and arranged for transportation. These included Smith Corners and Rensselaerville west of Albany; Charlston, Four Corners and Quaker Street closer to Schenectady; and Easton northeast of the Tri-City area.

Albany had an active Vigilance Committee that began in the 1840s to protect fugitive slaves from re-enslavement and to provide legal aid, food, clothing, money, sometimes employment, temporary shelter and assistance in making their way toward freedom. A flyer circulated by the committee in 1856, soliciting clothing and support for fugitives, listed the local address of the committee office and the names of members. This tells us that in contrast to the Underground Railroad's reputation for secrecy, the abolitionist movement had a more public side.

Stephen Myers, a former slave born in Rensselaer, was a leading spokesperson for antislavery activity and rights for African Americans. In his 1840s newspaper the *Northern Star* and *Freemen's Advocate*, he wrote about temperance, African American rights and the need to abolish slavery. He helped thousands of individuals to move through Albany to points west, north and east on the Underground Railroad. Myers noted that in one year he helped more than three hundred persons who came through Albany on their way to Canada or other points. In the 1850s, he was the principal agent of the Underground Railroad in Albany. Under his leadership, the Albany branch of the Underground Railroad was regarded by some as the best-run part in the whole state.[49]

In the 1850s, traffic on the Underground Railroad soared. Early in 1860, Stephen Myers declared that more fugitives had arrived in Albany in the past three years than in the six previous years. James Miller

Opposite: The Eastern Route map of the Underground Railroad of New York State. *Reprinted with permission from author Dr. William Switala from his book* Underground Railroad in New Jersey and New York.

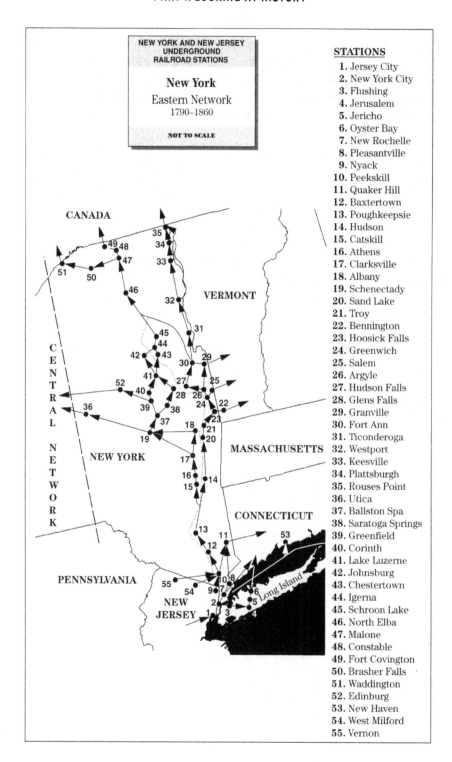

NEW YORK AND NEW JERSEY
UNDERGROUND
RAILROAD STATIONS

New York
Eastern Network
1790–1860

NOT TO SCALE

CANADA

VERMONT

CENTRAL NETWORK

NEW YORK

MASSACHUSETTS

CONNECTICUT

Long Island

PENNSYLVANIA

NEW JERSEY

STATIONS

1. Jersey City
2. New York City
3. Flushing
4. Jerusalem
5. Jericho
6. Oyster Bay
7. New Rochelle
8. Pleasantville
9. Nyack
10. Peekskill
11. Quaker Hill
12. Baxtertown
13. Poughkeepsie
14. Hudson
15. Catskill
16. Athens
17. Clarksville
18. Albany
19. Schenectady
20. Sand Lake
21. Troy
22. Bennington
23. Hoosick Falls
24. Greenwich
25. Salem
26. Argyle
27. Hudson Falls
28. Glens Falls
29. Granville
30. Fort Ann
31. Ticonderoga
32. Westport
33. Keesville
34. Plattsburgh
35. Rouses Point
36. Utica
37. Ballston Spa
38. Saratoga Springs
39. Greenfield
40. Corinth
41. Lake Luzerne
42. Johnsburg
43. Chestertown
44. Igerna
45. Schroon Lake
46. North Elba
47. Malone
48. Constable
49. Fort Covington
50. Brasher Falls
51. Waddington
52. Edinburg
53. New Haven
54. West Milford
55. Vernon

McKim quipped that the Underground Railroad was the "only branch of industry" that "didn't suffer" during the panic of 1857. "Other railroads are in a declining condition and have stopped their semiannual dividends but the Underground has never done such a flourishing business."[50]

With the advent of the Civil War, fleeing blacks no longer needed to reach Canada. Freedom was available at the nearest Union army post. By 1862, James Miller McKim could write, "An end is put…to the Underground Railroad….I take this opportunity…to thank the contributors to the treasury of the Philadelphia Vigilance Committee…and to notify them that in all probability we shall have no further call for their aid in this particular line of business."[51] As the decade drew to a close, enforcement of the Fugitive Slave Law became difficult in many parts of the North.

Henry Highland Garnet, an African American abolitionist minister, educator and outstanding orator, worked in the Troy, New York UGRR depot on the Hudson River—a natural way station along the Eastern Route of the Underground Railroad. He encouraged slaves to obtain their freedom through resistance. Philip Foner stated that Garnet claimed that he sent 150 runaways to safety annually.[52]

Abel Brown was a radical abolitionist and Baptist minister who was active in assisting fugitives in Albany, Troy and Sand Lake around the late 1830s and early 1840s. He was noted as an uncompromising and provocative individual who went to great lengths for the antislavery cause and was not at all secretive about it. He was a key figure in the operation of the abolitionist paper the *Tocsin of Liberty* (1842) (later known as the *Albany Patriot*), which published the annual report of the local vigilance committees, notes on antislavery meetings in Washington and Schoharie Counties and notes on the progress of the Liberty Party, as well as stories from other antislavery papers.

In April 1841, Abel Brown became the pastor at the Sand Lake Baptist Church. The Albany area was well suited for his antislavery work since, according to a biographical memoir published by Brown's second wife, Catherine, after his death in 1849, this was

a city which from its location on the banks of the Hudson, was the constant resort of fugitive slave, when travelling [sic] in the direction of the North Star, to seek shelter under the wings of Queen Victoria's dominion, or happily, perchance, to find an Asylum in the nominally free States.[53]

There are numerous documented safe houses from Albany and Troy to the Town of Chester, in East Greenbush, Greenwich (formerly Union Village), Sand Lake, Moreau, Glens Falls and Warrensburg and north from the Town of Chester to Schroon Lake, Keeseville, North Elba and Peru, New York.

Some passengers arrived by boat using the Hudson and Schroon Rivers (or nearby footpaths), which merge in Warrensburg and form the borders of the Town of Chester. The suspected Warrensburg safe house was in fact a livery station right on the Schroon River, which allowed runaways to arrive at night by boat and leave quickly by wagon, on horseback or on foot the next day.

The Wesleyan Methodist Church Warrensburgh Class broke away from the existing Methodist Episcopal Church, which it believed did not take a strong enough stand against slavery. With a land transfer in 1855, it became a part of the Town of Chester and was simply the Darrowsville Wesleyan Methodist Church. The church was originally founded in 1843 by congregants who supported relief for fugitives in their midst.

The significance of the presence of a group of abolitionists in the Town of Chester was duly recognized as early as 1845. In June of that year, Gerrit Smith toured the region and stopped in Chestertown to "preach politics" at the First Presbyterian Church on Main Street, which still stands in a greatly altered condition. He declared, "I am much pleased with this people. They are candid and truth loving. Their ministers are not ashamed, nor afraid, to plead the cause of the enslaved. Here are abolitionists of the truest class."[54]

2.

TOWN OF CHESTER HISTORY

*T*he Town of Chester is located in Warren County, New York, near the southeastern corner of the Adirondack Park. It is along State Route 9 at the foothills of the Adirondack Mountains. It was first settled about 1789 and set off from the Town of Thurman on March 25, 1799.[55] The town comprises the main villages of Chestertown and Pottersville, as well as several outlying settlements and two lakes, Friends Lake and Loon Lake. Ideally located between the east and west branches of the Hudson River, it was possible to enter the virgin territory by boat, the pioneer's easiest method of transportation.

Much of the wilderness was already familiar to men who had fought in the colonial wars, and some of the families who first moved into the Gore area had already been given colonial grants prior to the revolution. After the Revolutionary War, many of the soldiers were given several hundred acres as payment for their services. Quakers from Dutchess County and Moreau were also among the early settlers.

The main settlement was known as Chester Four Corners, or simply Four Corners. When the first post office was established there on June 27, 1808, this settlement became known as Chestertown to distinguish it from Chester in Orange County.[56] Gabriel Fox was the first postmaster.

Shortly after the Revolutionary War, Seba Higley secured a piece of land on what is now Landon Hill, which he purchased in 1801. From the Higley family history one learns that he walked back and forth from his dwelling in Hebron to the hill. He made a clearing and put up a log house and did planting in 1810 before he finally returned with his family. When Warren County was established on March 12, 1813, Seba Higley was chosen as the first supervisor of the Town of Chester in the new county.

By the 1830s the town had grown into two main settlements, Chestertown and Pottersville, with several smaller ones. The first post office in Pottersville, the second-largest village, was established on December 5, 1839. The first postmaster was Joel F. Potter, for whom the village was named. Darrowsville was named after James Darrow; Starbuckville took its name from James Starbuck. Landon Hill was named after M.B. Landon, who ran a tavern at the foot of the hill. There was also Igerna and part of Riverside.

The early economy centered on farming, lumbering and tanning. On some farms there were men with special skills—millers, blacksmiths, carriage makers, tinsmiths and shoemakers. By 1835 the village of Chestertown had a gristmill, a sawmill, a clothing factory, three blacksmith shops, an academy, two taverns, three stores and about 150 dwellings.[57] In the archives of the Town of Chester Historian is found the following: In 1845 the population of Chester was 1,608; there were sixteen common schools, four church buildings and nine clergymen, who were paid cash. The improved land in town totaled 11,951 acres. Production that year was 50,036 pounds of butter, 11,990 pounds of cheese, 31,176 bushels of potatoes, 32,252 bushels of wheat and 20,372 yards of pulled cloth.

Alexander Robertson built the first tannery in Chestertown in 1849, more commonly known as C.H. Faxon & Son. Charles H. Faxon was in the business from the beginning, as the firm was Robertson, Faxon & Company. William Mundy built a small tannery at Friends Lake. There was also a tannery in Pottersville, at various times known as Fraser-Major, Milton Sawyer and Fay & Company. That tannery later became a cider mill.

From its earliest days, the town's greatest natural wonder was the stone bridge and its caves near the northern end of town. This bridge is described in Morse's *Geography* of 1790 as follows: "In the County of Montgomery is a small, rapid stream emptying into Schroon Lake, west of Lake George; it runs under a hill, the base of which is 60 to 70 yards in diameter, forming a most curious and beautiful arch in the rock, as white as snow. The fury of the water and the roughness of the bottom, added to terrific noise within, have hitherto prevented any person from passing though the chasm." This is Natural Stone & Caves in Pottersville, a major tourist attraction for the town.

The Town of Chester had common schools beginning in 1789. In 1820 there were seven districts, which kept school an average of five months a year and taught 224 pupils. There were also several select schools and the Chester Academy, which preceded the graded school system.[58] High schools were the natural outgrowth in both Pottersville and Chestertown. Consolidation of districts happened quickly in the late 1920s and early 1930s. Both villages built centralized schools. Further consolidation occurred in the early 1970s, when Pottersville, Chestertown and Horicon Central Schools formed the North Warren Central School District.

The first church in the town was the Baptist church, which was organized in 1796 in Chestertown, with Reverend Jehiel Fox as the pastor. In Pottersville the Methodists formed a society in 1810 and erected a house of worship in 1847. Today that building is the Pottersville United Methodist Church and continues to hold worship services. One of the first Wesleyan Methodist Churches in the state was organized on July 14, 1843, in Darrowsville. The church was built in 1845 and became a stop on the Underground Railroad. At various times the town has had Baptist, Methodist, Wesleyan Methodist, Presbyterian, Lutheran, Dutch Reformed, Episcopalian, Roman Catholic, Quaker, Christian Scientist and interdenominational groups.

Very early on, Chester became a mecca for summer visitors, and the tourist trade became part of the economy of the town. In 1898 the Souvenir Edition of the *Warrensburgh News* described the area as "A Thriving Adirondack Village Where Balsam Laden Air Is Attracting Thousands." Many hotels, boardinghouses and summer resorts sprang up to care for these visitors. Early travelers made the journey by the D&H Railroad to the Glen Station or the Riverside Station. From the station, travelers could take stages to their destination. Later, an autobus, known simply as "the Auto," carried passengers from the train. As travel became easier and more affordable, summer resorts were built on Friends Lake and Loon Lake, which offered accommodations as well as many activities for their guests.

The Town of Chester continues to attract vacationers today. Recreational opportunities in the area have expanded to include cross-country skiing and hiking trails, continuing development of park land at Dynamite Hill and a joint effort with the state and Warren and Essex Counties to develop the former Scaroon Manor site along the shores of Schroon Lake. There are also many seasonal homes surrounding Friends Lake and Loon Lake, as well as various accommodations for visitors.

Transportation

Traveling in the early part of the nineteenth century was difficult. Roads were mostly widened dirt paths, probably following trails left by Indians, trappers and soldiers from the Revolutionary War. People traveled by foot, horseback, horse and wagon or by stagecoach.

At the time of Gerrit Smith's antislavery tour, there is no record of how he traveled north from Albany. Most likely it was by stagecoach or horse and wagon. By the dates in his writing we can see the time involved in traveling from Saratoga Springs to Plattsburgh. He leaves Saratoga Springs on May 26, 1845, and ends his narrative in Plattsburgh on June 16. He reaches Elizabethtown the evening of June 4. At five o'clock in the morning of June 5, he left for "Keene Plains," about twenty-five miles west of Elizabethtown. He returned the evening of June 6, "having traveled between 50 and 60 miles—22 of them on foot—and a part of the 22 over mountains."

The Plank Road

In the early 1800s, in what was to become Warren County, the roads, mostly Indian trails, were in a primitive state and hard to navigate except on foot or horseback. They were full of stumps, rocks and ruts. While we may not know specifically where these old trails were, we know that many of them became the early plank roads and the highways of today. Before 1882 the only public transportation was by stagecoach. Although there were stops in northern Warren County, stagecoaches were not widely used until the late 1860s.

The plank road sign is in the Museum of Local History of the Town of Chester. *Courtesy Laura Seldman.*

On May 7, 1847, the New York State Senate and Assembly amended the Plank Road Act, Chapter 210 of the laws of 1847, "to provide for the incorporation of companies to construct plank roads, and of companies to construct turnpike roads." The Glens Falls and Lake George Plank Road Company was organized, and in 1848 a plank road was laid from Glens Falls to Lake George along the route of the military road. In 1849 that road was extended from Lake George to Warrensburgh. The original Warrensburgh and Chester Plank Road Company was organized on January 9, 1850, and the road was extended from Warrensburgh to Chester along what is now Route 9. In March 1871, the name was changed to the Warrensburg-Chester Plank Road and Turnpike Company. The plank road followed the old stagecoach road that began at Albany and ended at the Canadian line. With few exceptions, that became the present-day Route 9.

Due to its strength and slow rate of decay, plank roads were generally constructed of hemlock. A plank road was laid by first placing parallel lines of timbers called stringers. These were usually three by twelve inches and laid about six inches apart. Two sets of stringers were needed and were laid about three or four feet apart along a graded surface. Then heavy boards or planks, three by six inches, were laid crossways over the timbers. The heavy weight of the planks kept them in place. The planks could be up to twenty-four feet in length but were more commonly sixteen to eighteen feet. This amounted to an estimated 160,000 board feet of lumber per mile. That would be around two million board feet for the twelve-mile road from Warrensburgh to Chester. The Woodward sawmill, located near Millington Brook in what is now Pack Forest, supplied much of the timber for the Warrensburgh section. The labor for laying a single track of stringers and planks included grading, turn outs and ditching. This would cost from fifty cents to one dollar per rod, which is sixteen and a half feet. There are 320 rods per mile, so the labor cost would be $160 to $320 per mile, or up to $4,000 for the twelve-mile section from Warrensburgh to Chestertown. The actual cost for construction of the Warrensburgh to Chester Plank Road was $18,000.

New York State law decreed that plank roads were to be at least four rods (sixty-six feet) wide, bedded with gravel or stone and with ditching on both sides. The arch or bed of the road for a turnpike had to be at least eighteen feet wide to allow for vehicles to pass. Once the road was finished, it was inspected, and a certificate of approval was issued. Then toll gates could be constructed, not closer than three miles apart, and fares for using the plank roads and turnpikes were set. The toll gate between Warrensburgh and Chester was located just south of the intersection of today's Routes 9 and 28. Toll rates for the plank road were set at a maximum of one and a half cents per mile for vehicles drawn by two animals, with one-half cent per mile for each additional animal. For vehicles drawn by one animal, the rate was three-fourths of a cent per mile. A horse and rider or a led horse cost one-half cent per mile. The maximum rate for a score of swine, sheep or neat cattle was one cent per mile.[59]

At first the large, heavy stagecoaches provided a fairly smooth ride over the plank roads, but eventually the planks became warped and shrunk from exposure, leaving gaps between the planks, producing an annoying clatter. The plank roads were difficult to maintain and were never a financial success. But they did open up travel to northern Warren County.

Travel in the time of the Underground Railroad was most likely by foot, on horseback and maybe by farm wagon. It was neither an easy nor a quick journey to bring escaped slaves into the northern area of Warren County and beyond.

Chester to Canton Road

In 1967 Leslie Rist wrote a paper for the St. Lawrence Historical Society titled "The Chester to Canton Road." He was a member of the Historical Society of the Town of Chester at that time and gave a copy of his paper to that organization. The information in this section is mostly from his paper.

Incidents that occurred in the years preceding the War of 1812 led many Americans to believe that a war might materialize between the United States and Great Britain. In 1807 these incidents were especially disturbing to the people of New York State, who could be easily attacked from the southeast as well as from Canada, then garrisoned by British troops.

One of the results of the feeling that war might be imminent was the passing of an act by the New York legislature in 1807, "To Lay Out and Open a Road from the Town of Chester to the Town of Canton." But there was no mention in the wording of anything pertaining to the military. Alfred Donaldson's *History of the Adirondacks*, written in 1921, contains a chapter on military roads in which he mentions a central road from Chester to Russell. He states that this one was the earliest to be projected. Donaldson gives the course of this road as follows: "Starting at Chester it ran northwesterly into and through Essex County, following approximately the North Branch of the

Parts of the time-weathered unpaved roads are disappearing. Covered by moss and leaves, rock walls along the old military road near Perry House are now barely visible. *Courtesy Laura Seldman.*

Hudson River. It then turned to the west, passing through the northeasterly corner of Hamilton County, and crossing the outlet of Long Lake. Thence it passed into the extreme southwestern corner of Franklin County, and so into St. Lawrence County, skirting the southern end of Tupper Lake. After that it followed the general direction of the Grasse River to Russell." William McAlpine's *A Map of the State of New York 1808* shows the approximate route of this highway. The mileage from Chester to Russell was one hundred miles, and from Russell to Canton was twelve miles. There are conflicting statements as to exactly where this road began in Chester, but most likely it began in the northern end of the town, close to the border with Essex County. Other names for this route were the Old Lake George Road (as it was an extension or apparent extension of it), the State Road from Chester to Russell, the Old Vermont Road, the Road to Pendelton and the Old Military Road.

In 1970 Dr. Emil Kraeling wrote a series of articles for the *North Creek News Enterprise* entitled "The Mystery of the Chester-Canton Road." In regards to where exactly this road began, he says, "It is not clear whether there had been an old connecting road leading through what later came to be called 'Igerna.' Perhaps, nothing more than a path existed." On the west side of Loon Lake in the Town of Chester there is an abandoned road that leads past the Tyrell house, over the mountain behind that house and into Igerna. It connects to what is now Perry Road, goes past the Ethan Perry House and follows another abandoned road over Ethan Mountain and comes out on the Pottersville-Olmstedville Road. That road leads to Route 28N and is known locally as "the old military road." Both the Tyrell house and the Ethan Perry house were stagecoach stops on this road.

3

THE WELLMAN SCALE

*T*o provide a clearer picture of what the Underground Railroad looked like in its time and to aid researchers in evaluating particular sites today, Judith Wellman, professor emeritus of history at the State University of New York and president of Historical New York Research Associates, developed a five-point scale for evaluating and rating the likelihood that a claimed site was actually involved in the Underground Railroad. Her work in developing what has come to be known as the Wellman Scale was supported by grants from the National Park Service and the Preservation League of New York State.

The Wellman Scale is the definitive means for rating the likelihood that a site claiming Underground Railroad involvement actually was involved. It may also be used in rating Underground Railroad stories not involving sites. The Wellman Scale uses five ratings, from doubtful to conclusive, to estimate the likelihood of a site's Underground Railroad involvement.

Level 1
Story probably not true

Reason to doubt: a local oral tradition about the Underground Railroad with reason to believe that it is probably not true. Story assumed not true until proven otherwise.

Level 2
Story possibly true

No reason to doubt, but no evidence so far. Rating for sites and people linked to local stories about involvement with the Underground Railroad that sound reasonable yet lack corroborating evidence. Likely candidates include adult African Americans born in northern states and known members of abolitionist churches.

Level 3
Good chance the story is true

Abolitionist sympathies, abolitionism or African American background, but no direct evidence of Underground Railroad activity. Potential Underground Railroad affiliation backed by oral tradition and/or some evidence of abolitionist activity—that is, antislavery society membership, signatures on antislavery petitions or antislavery church membership. African American birth in the South or Canada suggests involvement.

Level 4
Story almost certainly true
Considerable evidence of involvement

Oral traditions related to specific sources or to groups known to be sympathetic to freedom seekers or evidence of direct involvement with the Underground Railroad. High probability of Underground Railroad involvement but lacking direct primary source evidence. Strong written evidence from others coupled with a strong oral tradition make a compelling case for Underground Railroad involvement.

Level 5
Story almost certainly true
Conclusive evidence of involvement

Persons or sites identified through oral histories or written sources corroborated specifically by at least one reliable primary source. Strong primary source evidence of Underground Railroad activity: stories about the Underground Railroad that are supported by a primary source recorded by someone who was actually involved. An obituary written by someone who knew the person may qualify as compelling evidence.

What remains today through the oral traditions of handed-down accounts and, in many fewer cases, actual documentation is precious but dwindling as oral traditions continue to die out with the passing of descendants of freedom seekers, safe house operators and conductors. Thus, it is vital to record and preserve Underground Railroad stories while they remain with us and to ensure that they are not forgotten.

About two-thirds of claimed Underground Railroad sites have a rating on the Wellman Scale of 2, "Oral tradition with no reason to doubt." These sites are thus the heart of the Underground Railroad.

Only 4 percent of claims have been able to be substantiated with documentation and receive a Wellman Scale rating of 5 since July 2008, when the scale was created.

As we review the information we have for each site, we are challenged to accurately rate each one according to the Wellman Scale.

4.

OUR BEGINNING

Darrowsville Wesleyan Methodist Church

The Darrowsville Wesleyan Methodist Church was located three miles south of Chestertown on Dennehy Road. It was part of a thriving community known as Darrowsville. In February 1843 there was a preliminary convention held at Andover, Massachusetts, that approved the formation of local Wesleyan Societies pending the establishment of a general organization. This split in the Methodist Church, known as the Great Schism, was caused by the disagreement between those who protested slavery and the use of alcoholic beverages and wanted that to be the prime focus of the church and those who saw no reason to change. A great convention was called in Utica, New York, on May 31, 1843, and the Wesleyan Methodist Connection was formed. The Wesleyan discipline differed considerably from the Methodist Episcopal Church in that it prohibited slaveholding and the use of intoxicating beverages.[60] That same year, on July 14, 1843, the Wesleyan Methodists at Darrowsville were organized. It is reputed to be one of the first churches organized after the formation of the Wesleyan Connection. It was first known as the Warrensburgh Class. In 1855, by an act of the Warren County Board of Supervisors, a one-mile strip of land from the Schroon to the Hudson Rivers was taken from the Town of Warrensburgh and given to the Town of Chester.[61] Afterward the church is listed in records as the Darrowsville Class. Thomas Baker and Myron Tripp helped to organize the Wesleyan Methodist Church at Darrowsville

This undated vintage photograph shows the Darrowsville Church as part of the community of Darrowsville. *Courtesy Historical Society of the Town of Chester Archives.*

and later to build the church structure. Reverend John Wood was the first pastor until 1845. He is buried at the Darrowsville Cemetery.

In *The Underground Railroad from Slavery to Freedom,* written in 1898 by Wilbur H. Siebert, Mr. Siebert says, "Indeed, it came to be said of the Wesleyans, as of the Quakers, that almost every neighborhood where a few of them lived was likely to be a station of the secret Road to Canada."

The Darrowsville Wesleyan Methodist Church building was erected in 1845 on an acre of land obtained from Orange Woodhouse by a deed dated June 16, 1845. This would hold the church building and an adjacent cemetery. The building was a white frame structure with a simple bell tower housing a 3-foot bell.[62] It is not known what happened to that first bell. In 1895 a bell from Rumsey & Company, Limited, in Seneca Falls was installed in a larger, added bell tower. The 3-foot bell cost $37.50.[63] The building was 28 feet by 23.5 feet and could seat 150 people. There was no plumbing and no electricity, and the only heat it had was from a potbellied wood stove. The church and a parsonage were built on the Wood homestead. The parsonage was destroyed in a fire in 1850, and the early church records were lost. The trustees of the church later sold the property where the parsonage had stood.

Another church at Darrowsville, the Methodist Episcopal Church, was organized in 1856. This church did not survive and by 1876 had disappeared.

Reverend Thomas Baker was the second pastor and the first abolitionist pastor of the Darrowsville Church. It is believed that he hid fugitive slaves in the parsonage. According to an obituary written for Eunice Baker, the Reverend Baker's widow, Thomas Baker was well known throughout northern New York for his identification with the antislavery movement.[64]

Another abolitionist pastor who served the Darrowsville Wesleyan Methodist Church was Reverend S.H. Foster.[65] He was a staunch abolitionist and served many churches throughout northern New York and one in Vermont. He served as pastor of the Darrowsville Church three separate times. He married Jane Ann Tripp, a local girl. Their son Matt Foster married Julie Oliviere, another local girl, who afterward gained fame as Jeanne Robert Foster, a writer and poet of the early 1900s.

Reverend S.H. Foster died in 1893. He and his wife, Jane, are buried at Chester Rural Cemetery.

In 1897 the membership of Darrowsville was united with the Brant Lake Church. The Darrowsville charge continued, and regular services were held until 1930. Services were then held intermittently, mostly in summers, until 1937. There were two attempts, which failed due to lack of attendance, to revive services in 1940 and 1954. The church sat abandoned after that. There were two attempts to restore the church, one in 1976 and one in 1982. But the question of ownership of the church arose. The original 1845 deed was the only known deed; there was never any deed found to divide the church property from the original property. The Wesleyan Methodist organization gave the church to the Town of Chester in 1976, but there was never any legal paperwork filed. In 2011 the Historical Society of the Town of Chester obtained a quit claim deed to the church and the adjacent cemetery. Over the years the church had lost its roof, and one side had partially collapsed. In 2012 it was deemed unsafe and was deconstructed. Plans were made to build a memorial on the footprint of the original church and relocate the bell in housing made from church timbers. Fundraising began, and those plans were realized by 2016, with storyboards that tell the story of the hamlet of Darrowsville and its role in the Underground Railroad.

The Darrowsville Memorial is located a short distance from the intersection of Route 9 and Dennehy Road. Drive past the sawmill and you will see the memorial and cemetery on your right. There is a handicap parking space and benches to sit on. You can read the story of this important settlement and its crucial role in the Underground Railroad movement.

Thomas Baker

Thomas Baker was born about 1809, the son of Peleg and Sally Baker. He married Eunice Harris of Athol, who was brought up by her grandmother

Elizabeth Warren, before 1830. He first appears in the 1830 Federal Census in the Town of Warrensburgh living next to his father, Peleg. He also appears in the 1840 Federal Census in Warrensburgh with his wife and an older woman, most likely his mother. Before the 1850 census, only the head of household was listed by name. Beginning in 1850, all members of a household were listed.[66] In 1850 Thomas and Eunice Baker are again listed in the Town of Warrensburgh, this time with daughter Julia A. During the time of these three censuses the area of Darrowsville was in the Town of Warrensburgh. In 1855, a one-mile strip of land that included Darrowsville was given to the Town of Chester. It is most likely that Thomas Baker and his family lived in or near the settlement of Darrowsville from 1830 until 1854, when they moved to Minerva. Thomas had two daughters: Jennie, also known as Jane, and Juliette, also known as Julia.

Reverend Thomas Baker was the second pastor of the Darrowsville Wesleyan Methodist Church. It is believed that he hid fugitive slaves in the church parsonage, which was located near the church. For reasons unknown, Thomas Baker; his wife, Eunice; and their twelve-year-old daughter Julia left Darrowsville and moved to Minerva in 1854. He purchased the property later known as the North Woods Club.[67]

The July 19, 1968 edition of the *Essex County Republican News*, published in Keeseville, New York, contains a column entitled "Mountain Laurel" written by Billie Allen. In that issue she writes about the Underground Railroad in northern New York. She states that Emily McMasters was a productive source of information for her. She quotes parts of a letter she received from McMasters as follows:

We know so little of the Underground Railroad. They came from the south—the deep south—Kentucky and Tennessee seeking freedom into the North. They reached Philadelphia and New Jersey. Then they went on to New York and up the Hudson into northern New York—Essex, Franklin and Clinton counties. Washington county, too, which seems to have been one of the most traveled routes. There were quite a number of stations where the runaway slaves found food and lodging: Salem, Argyle, a number in Greenwich, one in Hudson Falls (Sandy Hill), Kingsbury....

A Reverend Thomas Baker lived in Minerva many years ago, at one time a Wesleyan minister at Chestertown. He preached against slavery and helped John Brown smuggle slaves into Canada. The story goes that the slaves were brought from near Lake George to Darrowsville where the

Reverend hid them and fed them. When they were rested they were taken back of Schroon Lake to New Russia, then on to John Brown's home in North Elba, and thence to Canada.

Emily McMasters was a noted area historian in Clinton County. She was a member of the Clinton County Historical Association and curator of its museum. She died in 1972.

William L. Stone of Jersey City Heights wrote an obituary of Mrs. Thomas Baker in 1891. In it he says:

I refer to Mrs. Thomas Baker, the widow of the last Rev. Thomas Baker, who, for many years, was well known throughout the whole of Essex and Warren Counties…and, indeed, through all of Northern New York, by his identification with the anti-slavery movement; and many times when I have been watching with him for deer in the silent watches of the night, on a "run-way" in some silent mountain pass, have I been encouraged and edified by his supreme faith in the ultimate freedom of the slave. His firm convictions in this regard and his effective eloquence both in the pulpit and on the stump made him universally respected even by those who were his bitter political enemies; and when he died at his woodland home, near the banks of the Boreas, a large concourse of neighbors and friends followed his remains to Chestertown, where he now rests after a "fight well fought and a course well finished."[58]

Thomas Baker died on November 3, 1863; his wife, Eunice, died on March 10, 1891. They are both buried at the Darrowsville Cemetery.

First Presbyterian Church

In 1845 Gerrit Smith undertook an antislavery tour through the northern counties of New York State. The journal he kept of that tour was reported in the June 25, 1845 edition of the *Albany Patriot*, an abolitionist newspaper published in Albany, New York. On June 2, 1845, Gerrit Smith arrived in Chester in the morning and spoke on slavery at the First Presbyterian Church in the afternoon.

The Presbyterian congregation in Chester was founded in 1806. The Presbyterians first met in the original schoolhouse located at the site of today's former Methodist parsonage on Route 9, just north of the present-day Chestertown Mini Mart. For many years they also sometimes met at the Baptist meetinghouse and on occasion in private residences. In 1821 the church was organized and joined the Troy presbytery, but it united with the classis of the Dutch Reformed Church in 1824. In October 1828, it returned to the Presbytery of Troy. On November 17, 1831, in the house of Ezra B. Smith, a group incorporated the First Presbyterian Church and Society of the Town of Chester. Orison Mead was the moderator.[69] The trustees elected at that time included Ezra B. Smith, whom Gerrit Smith names as an abolitionist "of the truest class." In 1843 William Hotchkiss, another abolitionist, appears as an elder in the church. Perhaps the connection of these men to that church was why it was the place chosen for Gerrit Smith's antislavery talk. From Smith's journal we learn that he spoke at other Presbyterian churches on his tour.

Presbyterian Church abolitionists arranged for Gerrit Smith to speak here in 1845. *Courtesy Historical Society of the Town of Chester Archives.*

The Presbyterian church building in Chester was originally constructed in 1833. So although the church was founded in 1806, when Gerrit Smith spoke there, this building was only twelve years old. It had a façade set out with several smaller spires around a lofty center spire. In its original design the building had two aisles and two windows at the back.

The First Presbyterian church of Chester was dissolved at its own request on September 17, 1918. It was declared extinct by the Presbytery of Troy, and the property was sold to Vetter's Hardware, the building just north of the church, and used by that company for storage and a showroom. The church building still stands, in an altered condition, as Butinno's Bistro. The house on the south side was the Presbyterian Manse.

Part II
FOUND

5.

UNDERGROUND RAILROAD SITES

*A*lthough the current owners have consented to be interviewed and have their homes described here, they wish to keep their exact locations private.

The Leggett Homestead and Joseph Leggett

The Leggett family in the Town of Chester began with Charles Leggett. Charles was born on September 16, 1761, in Newcastle, Westchester County, within the present bounds of New York City. He was the son of Isaac and Hannah Wiggins Leggett. Charles and his wife, Phoebe Willson Leggett, along with their seven oldest children, settled in Chester about 1796 or 1797.

Although many of the Leggetts were Quakers, this Charles, at one time, belonged to the British army stationed in America. The following story comes from a granddaughter of Nancy, Charles Leggett's sister. In 1917 the granddaughter, Alice Sanford, related that her grandmother had been greatly surprised when her brother Charles had appeared at her home about the time of the outbreak of the Revolution in the gray garb of a Quaker instead of the red uniform of a British soldier.[70]

At some point Charles moved from Westchester to Saratoga County. Family lore says that at one time during the war, he and his cousins were captured by Burgoyne's Indians, but when they were taken into camp the general ordered them released since they were noncombatants. It is believed that Leggett property was included in the Saratoga battleground and that Burgoyne's surrender took place on Charles's land.

Charles bought about two hundred acres of land from John Thurman for $450. The deed was not given until the state legislature passed, on March 25, 1800, "An Act for the Relief of John Thurman and Other Purposes." From this it would appear that early settlers in the area had no legal claim to their land for some time.

We learn about the history of the Leggett Homestead from a paper written by Helen Janette Leggett, great-granddaughter of Charles Leggett, in 1964.

Charles built a log house on the site of the present home. That house burned down a while later. The story is that the fire was caused by hams being smoked in the fireplace. The parents and younger children were away at the time, but the blaze could have been extinguished at the start had not someone kicked over the bucket of water in the excitement.

A log replacement was built on the approximate site of the central part of the present house. Later, a one-and-a-half-story frame addition was built where the original log house had burned. That still remains the west end of the house. The location of that original log house was discovered in 1939, about 140 years after the fire. There was no cellar under that part of the house, so one was excavated in 1939. This excavation brought to light charred fragments of the original log house.

A vintage Leggett family photograph shows a carriage when the road passed alongside the house. *Courtesy Leggett family collection.*

The replacement of the first building was moved a short distance to the south and, for a time, served as a home for Charles's eldest son, Willson, and his family. When they moved away it was used as a shop. Dr. Benjamin Franklin Leggett, author and educator and grandson of Charles, remembers playing there.

When this log structure was removed from where it had replaced the original, a one-and-a-half-story frame unit was built and attached to the similar part erected earlier on the site of the fire. This remains as the central portion of the present house. Originally the roof sloped unbroken from ridge to eaves, as that of the adjoining part still does, and the low windows of the upstairs room opened beneath a porch. That was changed long ago. Later a dormer was built on the north side.

Joseph W. Leggett, seventh son of Charles, was two years old when his family moved to Chester. When Joseph married Elizabeth Mead in 1830, a third and final portion of the present house was built. That "new" part is the two-story section facing the road. Sometime in its history it was modernized by the addition of a porch across the entire front. That was removed some years ago to restore the original design.

Only minor changes have been made in the appearance of the homestead. The old small pane windows were replaced with two-pane sashes. And the south porch was enclosed and, later, a wall removed to make it a part of the living room that adjoins it.

Charles was a surveyor and an agent for John Thurman, surveying and selling. In an old account book of his, on a page dated 1804, he lists charges of $1.50 per day for surveying. This was what a laborer, working with a team of oxen, received. Some of Charles's surveying chains remain in the family.

John Thurman held title to an extensive amount of land in this area. Frequently payments to Charles were made in produce. The need for storage of these "payments" is given as the reason for the large barns and the big building that stand northwest of the house. The huge hand-hewn beams were joined by wooden pegs and appear able to outlast several more generations.

When Charles died in 1834, his son Joseph received title to the homestead by his will dated June 12, 1832. The document served its purpose even though it simply lay around the house for 104 years until his great-great grandson of the same name had it recorded in 1936.

Joseph Leggett, a Quaker like his father before him, was born on December 25, 1794. He was the seventh son of Charles and Phoebe (Willson) Leggett. He married Elizabeth H. Mead in 1830. They had eight children, five boys and three girls.

The Leggett home is seen on a glorious Adirondack fall day in 2015. *Courtesy Laura Seldman.*

Above: Hand-colored tintype by an unknown photographer of Joseph Leggett recently found in a Leggett homestead dresser drawer. *Courtesy Laura Seldman.*

Opposite: Elizabeth Leggett joined her husband, Joseph, when he met with outspoken abolitionist Abel Brown at the Temperance Tavern. *Courtesy Laura Seldman.*

It was during Joseph's time that the Leggett homestead, just south of Chestertown, became a station on the Underground Railroad. Joseph was a leading abolitionist in the village, and his son Benjamin (the Dr. Benjamin Leggett mentioned earlier) remembered "glimpses of the escaping slaves."[71] Gerrit Smith, the leader of the antislavery Liberty Party in New York, visited Chestertown in 1845 and wrote this about its citizens: "I am much pleased with this people. They are candid and truth loving. Their ministers are not ashamed, not afraid, to plead their cause of the enslaved. Here are abolitionists of the truest class. I refer to such worthy men as Mr. Leggett, Mr. Arnold."

Joseph Leggett was the earliest abolitionist on record from Warren County. In 1836 he was listed as an agent for the New York City–based abolitionist newspaper, the *Emancipator*. In 1838 he was a participant at a state abolitionist convention in Albany. He and his wife dined at Oliver Arnold's Temperance with two Liberty Party lecturers in 1843, the Baptist abolitionist Reverend Abel Brown and Lewis Washington, a fugitive slave who often shared the podium with Reverend Brown. Joseph Leggett was president of the Liberty Party in Warren County in 1846.

Leggett was well known locally as an Underground Railroad conductor, as evidenced by mentions in area newspapers near the turn of the century. The March 10, 1898 edition of the *Ticonderoga Sentinel*, in Ticonderoga, Essex, New York, has this report on page three: "Miss Legett, who has been visiting friends about town recently, is a granddaughter of Joseph Legett of slavery times, who acted in the capacity of conductor on the underground railroad starting in the southern states and terminating in Canada, and many a fugitive slave has he fed, clad and sent on his way rejoicing at dead of night."

Another account of his activities was reported in the *Schroon Lake Star*, "The Underground Railroad Stop," and can be read in the section on Schroon Lake.

Joseph W. Leggett died on April 1, 1871. His wife, Elizabeth, died on June 1, 1895. They are both buried at the Chester Rural Cemetery, also known as the Leggett Cemetery. They are in the older section at the southern part of the cemetery, which started as a Quaker burying ground. The cemetery was started on Leggett property by the Leggett family and was eventually turned over to the Town of Chester.

Barns were a necessary part of a successful farm, like that of the Leggetts. They were used for shelter of animals and as storage for produce and equipment. *Courtesy Laura Seldman.*

Charles and Phebe Leggett are also buried there. The funeral of Charles in 1834 marked the last service at the nearby Friends Meeting House.

Interview with Craig Leggett

When I was a young man, we would always talk about that this was the house history. My great-grandfather Joseph Leggett was a conductor on the Underground Railroad. The story has been passed down, the one place where they, the fugitives, were hid overnight was in a bit of a tool room that was accessible from the outside. From the inside it backed up to a pantry, and so if you are looking at the house, you just never really noticed that it is connected to anything within the house.

The driveway rode up close, the carriage track was between the house and the woodshed. We have a picture of a horse-drawn carriage with family members sitting on the porch.

Any family stories? [Long pause]…No. No stories you can pin historical fact onto. We talk and wonder about why did Joseph Leggett become an abolitionist? How did he get involved with being on the Underground Railroad? This was a remote area. Now he moved to this area when he was about three years old, in the late 1700s, born 1794.

What was it like in the town to be able to create such fervor, to be able to put your property at risk because you're harboring stolen property.

What I wonder is, they started out as Quakers when they came up here, then he converted to Methodist; but why? There used to be a Quaker meetinghouse at some point. I have an old ledger book that I believe was related to the old Quaker meetinghouse.

So you have so much happening down Darrowsville two miles down the road, so how does that affect the rest area of the neighbors?

As a young teen I found a door behind a secretary where I discovered a musket, surveyor's instruments and an old wood stove. Joseph's father was a surveyor for John Thurman. I still have some links and chains. As kids we always thought the little wooden door to the side of the fireplace, underneath the stairs, was a secret place.

We really don't have any written communications directly from Joseph being a political activist. There must be a letter to somebody somewhere. After Joseph's death the cousins got together to decide. What is the future of the homestead? What could keep it going? They decided it is more suitable to be a home than to be a museum.

Oliver Arnold's Temperance Tavern

Oliver Arnold first appears in Chester in the 1820 U.S. Federal Census.

He is also in the 1830 and 1840 censuses in the Town of Chester. Before 1850 the census records list only the head of household and general ages and gender of members of that household. Besides Oliver, there appear to be his wife and younger males and females in his household in each of those censuses.

In the payroll abstracts for New York State Militia during the War of 1812, we find Oliver Arnold and Orison Mead. Mead was a captain in the company of Captain William Cook, Twenty-third Regiment. Arnold was a private in the same company. It is unknown whether Mead and Arnold knew each other before they served together or if that is where they met. But we know that both families ended up in the Town of Chester and became related by marriage.

The Temperance Tavern, now a private residence, is located on Landon Hill Road in Chestertown. It was built in the 1830s on land that Oliver Arnold bought in 1832 from Simeon Doty. Arnold had previously, in 1826, bought adjoining land from Lewis Numan, who married Polly Mead, the sister of his wife, Hannah. Oliver Arnold operated the building as a tavern, and it was a stopping place for stagecoaches on the route from New York to Montreal. In Gerrit Smith's antislavery tour, Arnold is mentioned as being an abolitionist "of the truest class." Oliver Arnold and his wife owned and ran the Temperance Tavern. Although it has not been proven that fugitive slaves were ever hidden there, it was a meeting place for local people who opposed slavery.

The house was built in layers over the years. When it was the Temperance Tavern, only the two front rooms existed, along with the two rooms on top of the first floor, with a double fireplace downstairs. Later, other rooms, including the kitchen and living areas, were added.

Oliver Arnold married Hannah Mead, daughter of Eli and Deborah Brush Mead. One of Hannah's brothers was Orison Mead, who was the moderator in 1831 when the First Presbyterian Church and Society of the Town of Chester were incorporated.[72] Ezra B. Smith was a neighbor of Arnold and the Temperance Tavern, since the land Arnold bought in 1832 bordered Smith's land.

Oliver Arnold was a staunch abolitionist, and while there is no evidence that the tavern was used to hide fugitive slaves, it was used for abolitionist meetings. He was very involved with the Warren County Liberty Party, serving as its secretary in 1841, when Joseph Leggett was president of that party. The tavern was a logical place to hold such meetings.

In 1841 Reverend Abel Brown helped establish the Eastern New York Anti-Slavery Society. In that same year Oliver Arnold is listed as vice-president of the society from Warren County, a Liberty Party candidate. In 1843–44 Abel Brown toured the Adirondacks. During this tour he frequently wrote letters to his wife describing his activities and surroundings. Reverend Brown passed away in 1844 while on this tour. In 1849 his wife, Catherine Swan Brown, published a *Memoir of Rev. Abel Brown., by His Companion, C.S. Brown.* This memoir included letters he

Visitors stopped for a rest or for something to eat at the Temperance Tavern. It was known to be used for antislavery meetings. *Courtesy Historical Society of the Town of Chester Archives.*

had written to her. The letter dated October 11, 1843, was written from the Temperance Tavern. He describes how busy he has been, but he is "now in a very quiet place in a Temperance house, (parlor very neat and comfortable)." In this letter he states he started in Albany, then went on to Schenectady, Ballston Springs, Corinth, Glens Falls, Sandy Hill and Caldwell. In each place, except Caldwell, he either had meetings or spoke at antislavery sessions. In Caldwell he was told, "there was no meeting, and only one Abolitionist within five miles." After some inquiries he did find someone to take him to an antislavery convention that was in session about five miles away in a Baptist meetinghouse. He does not mention exactly where that is. After he spoke there, he was taken to the residence of "Hon. Mr. Richards," who had invited him to spend the night there. The next day, he was "taken by my friend Leggett" and brought to Oliver Arnold's Temperance Tavern. He dined there with Mr. Leggett, who was the Warren County Liberty Party president, "and his Quaker wife, and am now writing at this Temperance house, at five o'clock and twenty minutes. The tea bell is ringing, and I must go to the table—then go to meeting and tell of the slaves' wrongs." He does not mention where

The Temperance Tavern house has been in Cathie Little's family for over one hundred years. *Courtesy Laura Seldman.*

that meeting was, but since it was early evening, we can assume that the meeting was probably in or near Chestertown.

When Gerrit Smith visited Chestertown in 1845 his journal states he arrived on June 2 and spoke at the Presbyterian Church in Chestertown on June 3. Though he doesn't mention where he stayed, it is probable that he stayed at the Temperance Tavern.

Oliver Arnold made his last will and testament in October 1844. In it he mentions his wife, Hannah, and his daughter, Mary Arnold. There is no mention of any sons or other daughters. After Oliver Arnold died on November 4, 1845, at the age of fifty-three, it is unclear if the tavern remained open. Arnold's will leaves his personal and real property to his wife, Hannah Arnold, with $100 to be paid to his daughter, Mary, when she becomes of age. Hannah Arnold died on December 25, 1845, less than two months after her husband, at the age of forty-nine. The assessment records for the Town of Chester show that the Oliver Arnold estate owed twenty-five acres in 1846, but there is no mention of it after that. Orison Mead and Melvin N. Mead were named executors of Oliver Arnold's will. Orison was a brother of Hannah Mead Arnold. In 1853 he was one of several people who sold Oliver Arnold's property to Milton Sawyer. In 1865 Joseph C. Thurston, an ancestor of the current owners, bought the property.

Oliver and Hannah were buried at the village cemetery, which used to be located on today's Theriot Avenue and later transferred to the Chester Rural Cemetery.

Over the years there were additions made to what began as a simple tavern, with two rooms up and two rooms down. Today it is a large, well-kept house and one of the most historic homes in the Town of Chester.

Interview with Cathie Little

This is a list of all the owners of my house. They were all my relatives, except the Sawyers. As you may know, my mother, Jane Parrott, was the town historian for some time. Mostly she put this list together. It would be interesting to know if it remained the Temperance Tavern and somebody else ran it after the death of Oliver Arnold in 1845. One of the things that we always heard being handed down through the family was that a previous owner, Oliver Arnold, had been second in command of an abolitionist society.

Well, other people claim that the basements or cellars were used in the story, but people use root cellars for food down there kept below the ground since it was always fifty-five degrees. It was a place to be if you were trying to avoid elements. There were reasons for building crawl spaces. Fifteen years or so ago, K_____ went under the house to rewire some electrical or tv cables. He was surprised to see the narrow crawl space get dramatically deeper toward the original part of the house. Sitting in that space rested a small-sized handmade wooden rope bed frame, child-sized but too big to have come through the crawl space.

My great-grandfather Andrew Chandler Thurston was an entrepreneur in the area, and it was his log mark in my kitchen. When you send the logs down the river you have to brand them with a hot iron to make a mark on them so that when they get down to where they're going everyone knows whose logs are whose. He's the one that put the shop on that wasn't on there before. There's a separate stairway that goes up to that area which would've been for the workers.

That was the shop that would've been on the second floor all the way in the back; that's where my great-grandfather used to make shoes and moccasins. I have read that he did it so that in the winter there would be

At the Little house, the porch was prepared for the oncoming storm. *Courtesy Laura Seldman.*

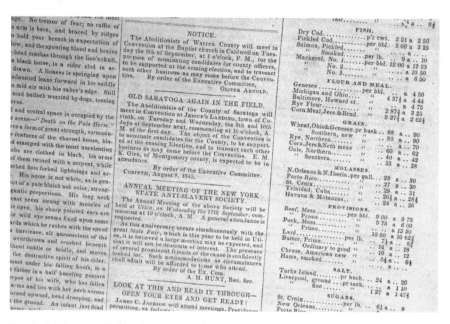

Proof of Oliver Arnold's antislavery involvement, this notice was printed in the *Albany Patriot* on September 9, 1845. Reprinted with permission from the New York Historical Society. *Courtesy Laura Seldman.*

work for the hired farm workers here. My parents donated the shoe form to the Adirondack Museum. So it's up there in storage.

So what they called the Temperance Tavern was a regular tavern as a stop on the New York to Montreal stagecoach. They had two rooms upstairs, one room was for the women and children to sleep in, the other was for the men to sleep. Downstairs on the town side is where they had like an open area, like a living room, parlor sitting room, kind of where everyone would get together. On the other side it was the dining room and kitchen, and then the stairs just went up between.

I think it was used as where one could just go to have something nonalcoholic because it was an eating and a gathering place, but also if you were on the stagecoach going through from New York to Montreal or vice versa you could stay there overnight.

You get into the basement crawl space from downstairs through one of the ten doors in the dining room.

That kind of thing to me is black-and-white; either you have proof or you don't have proof. It was part of in the sense that the people met there and, you know, discussed things, and therefore it was probably part of the Underground Railroad. Along with what you found about him being on the executive committee of the Liberty Party and owning the Temperance Tavern, that makes that connection; it puts it together.

Brayton-Dickenson-Carpenter House

The Brayton-Dickenson-Carpenter house was located south of Chestertown on the west side of what is now Route 9. In 1828 Levi Mead sold a parcel of land to John Brayton. In this deed, reference is made to Levi Mead's mill pond, which, at one time, was at the back of this lot. Levi Mead owned several parcels of land in the Town of Chester at that time, and there is no record of whether this parcel contained a house at the time of sale. John Brayton first appeared in the Town of Chester census records in 1830. In his household are one male (aged fifty to fifty-nine), one female (aged thirty to thirty-nine) and one female (aged forty to forty-nine). The land John Brayton bought from Levi Mead was the only piece of property for which there is a record of Brayton owning in the Town of Chester; the names before and after his in the census records indicate that this piece of land is where he lived.

In 1841 this property was sold to Samuel C. Dickenson. At that time the deed references John Brayton's residence. In 1845 Dickenson sold to Thomas Carpenter, who kept this land until 1863, when it was transfered to Joseph Carpenter. During the time of the Underground Railroad, this piece of property had three owners, John Brayton, Samuel Dickenson and Thomas Carpenter. There is no record of exactly when this house was involved in the Underground Railroad. Dickenson died in 1857 and is buried with his wife, Amy, at the Chester Rural Cemetery in Chestertown. Thomas Carpenter died in 1886 and is buried with his wife, Ursula, at the Chester Rural Cemetery.

In the early 1900s Harvey Tabor and his wife, Ester Hill Tabor, moved into this house. Their daughter Glennie was born there in 1901. Harvey Tabor, born about 1866, was the son of Alexander and Louise Tabor. About 1910 the Tabor family moved across the road to the east side of Route 9. In 1911 Harvey Tabor sold the house on the west side of Route 9 to Warren B. Hill, his father-in-law. In 1929 the house and land were deeded from Warren B. Hill to his son, Grant Hill and Grant's wife, Pansy. Grant Hill was a brother to Ester Hill, Harvey Tabor's wife. The current owner is the great-granddaughter of Grant and Pansy Hill. They acquired the house in the 1980s and are still living on the property.

According to family legend, the Grant Hill house sheltered slaves in the time of the Underground Railroad. *Courtesy Historical Society of the Town of Chester Archives.*

When they moved in, Glennie Tabor Sheldon was living in the house across the road that her father, Harvey Tabor, purchased about 1910. She visited the young family frequently and told them stories she had heard from her father and others about the house.

The original house was eventually demolished and the current one put in its place.

Interview with Barbara Davidson

The house was built in the 1800s. My great-grandfather was Grant and Pansy Allen, two owners. Grant's sister was a Tabor. The Tabor family was part of that because they lived in my house, and Harvey was Glennie's father. She did at some point live there.

The only thing I heard about the Underground Railroad was from Glennie Sheldon. About twenty-five years ago we got talking about our attic. I was kinda petrified of going up there, and I didn't care to go by myself. Anyways there were very, very narrow stairs. The house was almost like a boardinghouse. It had four or five bedrooms upstairs. The attic stairs was in the middle of all the rooms. It was narrow and it went up there. It was your third floor, one big room.

[Ms. Davidson paused, hesitated and apologized for having to speak an unacceptable ugly word.] *That was called "N_____'s heaven." That's why we believed that it probably had something to do with the transportation of the Negroes back then. So that's pretty much what she told me. I know she lived there and could tell me lots of stories.*

I saw one of the old pictures of the house. I wish I could find it. I know that I have seen it. Where Route 9 wasn't there, okay, and it was just a little dirt road, but you saw the whole property. You saw the big pond at that time, which now is kinda like swamp. It was a gorgeous lake, Glennie would tell me. And this is another thing, that if we did this nowadays we'd be arrested, but her mother would tie her to the tree with a rope and she could play in the yard but because the pond was so deep they were afraid she would run in. It's right beside my house. And there was a sawmill up behind there too on the north part of the property.

When the track was built across the road, all the silt filled in the two ponds. You used to be able to go fishing in a boat. I can remember almost 25 years ago probably that we could still go out on a boat and go trout fishing.

I had people telling me that we shouldn't tear the house down because it was historical. We couldn't afford to live in it, and my great-grandfather had told my parents when he gave them the property that they were to tear it down. But I could tell you it was a gorgeous home. You walked into the old kitchen; you had the pantry off to the right, because it's always where we got our cookies from my great-grandmother. The back of the house was a summer kitchen, then you had the main living room, bedroom, another living room, another room to the back of that, and then you went upstairs and saw the four to five bedrooms and then the little narrow staircase.

The tiny shed is all that remains from the original buildings.

William Tripp House

This property was in the hands of the Tripp family as early as 1809, when Albro Tripp purchased it from Everett Tripp. At that time he is listed as living in the Town of Thurman, Washington County, New York. This deed was filed in February 1824. Warren County was formed from Washington County in 1813.

Albro Tripp came to Chester from Rhode Island. His name first appears in the area when he purchases land in 1809. Family history says that Albro operated a small sawmill north of what is now Warrensburg in 1810 and that he had a farm in Chestertown. Warrensburg was set off from Thurman in 1813.

Payroll abstracts during the War of 1812 for New York State, dated 1812–15, tell us that Albro Tripp was a captain in that war. He was in the company of Colonel William Cook of the Twenty-third Regiment of the New York State Militia. This was the same company and regiment, at the same time, September 1814, as Oliver Arnold and Orison Mead. It is certainly possible that these three men knew one another before the time of the Underground Railroad movement.

Albro Tripp died in Chester May 1860 at the age of eighty-five. His son William B. Tripp died in Chestertown in February 1893, age eighty-five. He is buried at the Warrensburg Cemetery.

Albro and Amy Tripp were the parents of William B. Tripp, born in 1808, who owned the Tripp property in the 1830s. When the current owners were going through the house, they found an old book. On the inside cover of the book was William B. Tripp's name. He had written something that is now very hard to read, but part of what can be read says, "commenced house…on the…1832." In the archives of the Town of Chester Historian's office there is a single sheet of paper written in the 1980s that states that the "original house of Albro Tripp was located behind the current Tripp house." The land was all fields, and there was a path or wagon road that extended up the hill to another home and also extended to the north and over a definite bridge. It is believed that this was a stagecoach stop of the road from Albany to Montreal.

The present house has two cellars and a trapdoor leading into a small cellar room. It is believed that this house was used as a stop on the Underground Railroad.

Interview with Mr. S

William Tripp had a brother named Reuben. Reuben had a son who had a daughter named Lillian. Lillian married Melvin Baker. That's where Rachel, my grandmother, bought it from a descendant of that Baker. There is a question as to whether the property might have been listed in the Warrensburg land records in the 1840s.

The road that goes up toward our place had quite a few houses on it, and they probably would all have contributed to the school and the church. We've found four or five cellar holes with clay pipes and blue and white china pieces.

In the walls, we found candle molds, medicine bottles with medicine; part of it was for luck. I mean that they wanted good luck for their home, so they would take a bottle and they would put that in different places. And that was supposed to bring luck. We also found doll furniture that was handmade, letters, a child's shoe form and a pair of high-button shoes.

We found a rope bed up in the attic and an old, old book from 1832, adult wooden shoe forms, part of a shaker box and what I consider to be almost like a trophy: hand-forged chain that had been cut.

We found two frames in the barn. They were plaster cast frames. We took the frames apart and found the portrait drawings of a man and a

A length of chain was found in the attic of the Tripp house. Mr. S believes the cut chain was left by a fugitive slave. *Courtesy Mr. S.*

Mr. S found these two unknown portraits inside separate frames in the Tripp house barn. *Courtesy Mr. S.*

woman that had been used as the backings for other pictures. We wonder who they are. The pictures look like an actual photograph. I thought he was the abolitionist minister.

I know that there's a road that my dad might have referred to as the Stagecoach Road. There was a spot where we found old barrel staves.

Originally, the farm used to be called White Brook Farm. It was a boardinghouse. My folks [grandparents] *used to go up there for their vacations. In fact they had honeymooned on that property. When they could buy it, they did. My grandmother said they would come up from New Jersey. It was a gentleman's farm, which I guess had a couple pigs and "Old Boss," the cow. I had a horse when I was like eight or nine; I'd just ride up into the hills and not worry about nothing.*

It started as a two-room house; one for the bedroom, the other for everything else. They added an icehouse behind it, and then they added three barns, a chicken coop, and then one of the barns was replaced. We had a three-hole outhouse behind it; then eventually they added a sizable chunk to the main part of the house.

It's a real shame to see how everything went. When I inherited the house, it took so much to build it back, the cost was absolutely prohibitive.

The trapdoor that led to the hidden room in the basement of the Tripp house had always been covered by the living room rug. *Courtesy Mr. S.*

They didn't know that that room was there until I went to college. They decided to expand the cellar and then make it concrete, and when they pushed that wall it just caved in. They didn't expect there to be a void there. My dad said that there were very large shelves there which would've been the beds for the people. He said he thought it was unusual that they would have such a wide shelf, because it was so hard to reach the things at the back; but he wasn't into history at all and so consequently by the time I got there it was all thrown out. I do have a photograph of the trap door (which opened into the living room but was always covered with a rug). That cellar was scary dark, a perfect place for brown recluse spiders.

I love history.

The Hill House

This house is located on the west side of Friends Lake. It was part of the John W. Thurman estate. Thurman once owned a good deal of land in

Warren County, and it is thought that his great-nephew John R. Thurman initially owned the house. John R. Thurman was born in New York City in 1814, the son of Ralph Thurman, John W. Thurman's nephew. John R. graduated from Columbia College in 1835 and sometime after that moved to Chestertown. In 1838 he was living in the town of Chester and buying and selling land. In 1841 he married Sarah Tibbits Lane, daughter of Jacob L. Lane, in Troy, New York.

The earliest assessment records in the town historian's archives are for 1844. They show that John R. Thurman owned nineteen parcels of land in the Town of Chester at that time. John R. was a judge, held several local offices and owned a large farm. The 1850 Agricultural Census shows that he owned eight hundred acres of land, four hundred of which were improved and four hundred unimproved. His farm grew or produced wheat, rye, Indian corn, oats, peas and beans, Irish potatoes, buckwheat, butter and hay. His livestock consisted of horses, cows, oxen, other cattle, sheep and swine. He was elected as a Whig to the Thirty-first Congress in 1849 and served until 1851. His entry in the *Biographical Directory of the United States Congress*

Undated vintage photograph of Lyman Hill house. *Courtesy Historical Society of the Town of Chester Archives.*

says he declined to be a candidate for renomination in 1850 and turned his attention to the management of his estate in Chester. He died at his home on Friends Lake on July 24, 1854. He is buried at Oakwood Cemetery in Troy, New York.

The house, known locally as the Hill House, originally stood much farther back from the road and closer to Friends Lake; and it was smaller than it is now. Sometime in the mid- to late 1800s, it was moved to its present location. Thurman's caretaker was Sidney Hill. Sidney and his son Lyman worked for the Thurmans. In 1896 Lyman Hill bought the present house from Mary L. Thurman, daughter of John R. Thurman. Lyman Hill added the wings and the porch. He then opened it as a boarding house called the Hill House.

In 1974, Lyman Hill's daughter Cora gave a talk for the local historical society in which she stated that Ralph Thurman, John R. Thurman's father, had moved the house nearer to the road when he built a larger house on the original site. In a recently discovered undated document, which appears to be written by Cora Hill, we learned that "the cellar contained very large bake ovens—part of underground railroad."

The house and property are currently owned by Marion Eagan and her family. She is in the process of restoring the barns next to the house.

Interview with Marion Eagan

We bought the house in the 1960s. Our family was originally from Queens, and we came up to Friends Lake for weekends and summers. We were close to Cora, Cora Hill.

The house was used originally as a farm [Lyman Hill's farm], which came with a whole bunch of acreage on Friends Lake. When my grandmother bought it, it had been a boardinghouse, but it closed for years. It had twenty bedrooms with one bathroom, a huge basement and lots of outbuildings.

We purchased it because we had horses. The house we used to rent was right in the middle of this property, so when it came up for sale, we bought it. Since the house came completely furnished and because we didn't use the house, the place was vandalized. So we had an auction to sell off the contents, everything that was inside.

Many things in the house and on the property seemed a little bit, just different. This house sits back in the field. In the middle of that field in front, at some point, was a gazebo. We have pictures of it. Underneath that

The current owner plans to restore and update the original house, which will probably involve removing the two wings and adding modern plumbing. *Courtesy Laura Seldman.*

This page: Layers upon layers of wallpaper from two of the twenty bedrooms in the Hill House. *Courtesy Laura Seldman; courtesy Chloe Seldman.*

structure was dug out and lined with stones. Why did they do it that way? To this day in that field there's a circular indentation that has filled in and has not been excavated.

Last year we were cleaning out and fixing up the barns. Growing up I had not been back into this section of the property. I came across something that had a cover on it. It looked like a complete foundation for something built with stones. At one end was a rather large round area of stones, which was really curious to me. I found cooking utensils and stuff right in that general vicinity but no evidence of charring or ashes. Nobody has an idea what place this could have been. They had other places to store food. It was definitely hidden away and covered with roofing material, and it was absolutely level with the ground and it was in a tree-lined area. I had no idea it was just a very unusual spot to be in with five outbuildings.

Guests enjoyed the Adirondack-style gazebo at the Hill House in 1906. *Courtesy Historical Society of the Town of Chester Archives.*

The barn building down below from this had some very unusual storage. You could tell where the animals were. But the big, big space above did not have a staircase like the other barn did. Not something you would venture into.

The house was very interesting. The house had a complete standup height attic, and one section up there nobody had been in [since the 1960s]. There were storage boxes that looked like coffins. I always hated the attic. When you came down one side of the house into the kitchen, there was an opening in a wall that had a fake wall behind it. I remember I thought that area was for wood storage, until you saw that there was a second part behind it that went down to the basement. The basement had six rooms, with doors on all the rooms and a huge fireplace.

Lyman Hill purchased this property from Mary Lane Thurman in the late 1800s for $3,000. Town assessor records of 1850 show the barns being built in 1850. The barns were probably built first before the house.

Originally I found the powdered red paint; it was cheap and abundant, by the hundred gallons or so. You can still see the red paint in the section between two barns.

Above and opposite: At the Eagan property, the partially excavated "mystery hole" is bordered by stones of varied sizes and shapes. *Courtesy Laura Seldman.*

Top: Part of the restoration of the Hill House property has begun, with the rebuilding of the barns, originally built before the first house. *Courtesy Laura Seldman.*

Bottom: Found in the woods near the barns was an iron cauldron, or pig boiling pot. *Courtesy Laura Seldman.*

One of the six children, Nellie Mahoney, owned the small house in the corner of the property that I just redid. That piece Nellie sold to an architect, the architect built it, then Nellie bought it back.

I think that Hill House was not a boardinghouse for long. We do have the old register. They would pick up people from the Glen. This was an easy route if you wanted to get north of here; it was pretty direct. Further describing the house; there used to be a big stove in the dining room area; I found two hundred spindles from the front porch. When they left the house, they just left. I found an old cast-iron pig boiling pot, forged pieces and old traps. Old stone walls lined the road and crisscrossed the fields.

Cora Hill told us that this house was a stop on the UGRR.

Tyrell House

The Tyrell House is located on Loon Lake in the Town of Chester. It is known locally as the Tyrell House, as the Tyrell family owned it for over one hundred years.

Harvey Dickinson bought the property the house sits on in the 1830s. He also bought several other pieces of property. According to the town assessor's office, the house presently on this property was built in 1840. There was, in all probability, a smaller house already there when Harvey Dickinson bought the land. According to the Tyrell family, the stones from the original house were used to create a foundation for the back part of the house, which was part of the original home. In the 1850s the long part of the house was added.

Harvey Dickinson and his family first appear in the Town of Chester in the 1830 Federal Census. In the 1850 census, the first one to list the names of everyone in the household, Harvey has a wife, Patience, and two children, Mariette, age fifteen, and George, age eleven. Harvey died sometime between the 1865 New York State Census and the 1870 Federal Census. The Town of Chester assessment records show that

Vintage photograph of Mr. and Mrs. Clarence Tyrell found in the house. *Courtesy Baxter family collection.*

The original stories of the Underground Railroad at the property came from Clarence Tyrell, whose family owned the house for the longest period of time. *Courtesy Baxter family collection.*

George Dickinson is the owner of the property in 1869. The property leaves the Dickinson family in 1878, and in 1883 it is sold to Charles Tyrell. It remained in the Tyrell family until 1985, when Wayne and Sally Baxter bought it.

Mr. Tyrell's privacy notice. *Courtesy Laura Seldman.*

Like many of the early settlers in the town, Harvey Dickinson was a farmer. The 1860 Federal Census values his real estate at $1,400 and his personal estate at $620. Other than this, we know little about the Dickinson family. We know that the military road in this area went by his house and over the mountain to Igerna; his house was probably a stagecoach stop.

The Tyrell family owned the house and property the longest, and it is from them that the stories come. William Raidy, who sold the property to Wayne and Sally Baxter, inherited it from his wife, Alice Tyrell. Alice was the granddaughter of Charles Tyrell, who bought the place in 1883. Alice used to tell her husband stories about the house harboring slaves. Most of the basement of the house had been built with large heavy stones, but there was one small section that had been built with smaller stones. The story is that this was done because they were easy to remove, possibly for an entrance. When the Baxter family bought the house, this part of the basement had been sealed off from the rest, for heating purposes, and had not been used for many years.

While renovating their house, they discovered that the southeast corner of the front living room was not the corner of the house. From within, the view was of a wallpapered wall. Actually, there was a concealed room that could not be seen from within. The room was dismantled and disappeared in the rebuilding. The Baxter family has been able to save and preserve some of the items they found in the room, including the old quilt. So this Underground Railroad site has two places that could have concealed fugitive slaves—the basement and the hidden room.

Interview with Sally Baxter

We purchased the Tyrell farmhouse at Loon Lake, Chestertown, New York, in 1984. The seller, Mr. Raidy, inherited the house and property from his wife, Alice Tyrell. Alice Tyrrell couldn't marry Bill until her mother had passed away. Mr. Raidy told us she often told stories that the house had harbored runaway slaves on the Underground Railroad. I have Alice's diary from 1935, but it doesn't mention this.

Charles Tyrell was the father of Clarence [married to Elizabeth], *who we originally thought was the earliest owner we knew. Charles bought it from a man called Sherman Thompson about 1859–1860. I think that before that, the original people there were Meads. When I was in New York about six months ago, I came across some papers that my mother (she and Marge Swan) had compiled. There was a date of 1729 when there was a woman named Hannah and her child, a boy, were on that property, and I don't know if they were Indians or if they were related to the Meads.*

When we put the signs out by the road, we chose it to say 1760, because there is in that paperwork that the houses were there by 1760. The stones from the original house next to the well were used to create a foundation for the back part of our house, which was the original part of the house. In 1850 or 1860 they added the long part of the house. Charles's father's name was Ashile and his mother Anne Thompson. He was born in 1841 in Hebron. Those people that were his grandparents then would have been Anne's parents.

My mother said at one point the records for all of Warren were part of Washington County before 1813. On the original maps the Meads owned all of that.

Mr. Raidy gave me the 1905 picture of the house with the Thompsons when we bought the house.

To describe what it looked like when we first bought it: you came in the door here to the kitchen, the one lightbulb and cold running water. There were stone walls on both sides of the driveway.

They ran a bed-and-breakfast out of that house.

One day Wayne found a woman walking around the house; she was from Canada. She said she was writing a book about the Underground Railroad and she said "it is known throughout my area in Canada that this is documented that it's on the UGRR." Wayne didn't get a name.

Another time, maybe 1998, a group of black people came on a bus and motorcycles from Florida, yes. It could have been the freedom run. Since then there's been another man, Tom Calarco.

We were working on the house for probably over a year and one day my husband had finally got the middle part gutted down to the studs and he said to my son, "Well, we're going to have to move the stairs to do this or that." "Wait a second, dad. The house has three windows across the back. From the inside where is that window?" The window was boarded over. Everything was covered up with clapboards and they started pulling them off. There was no entrance to that room from inside the house. Our view from within was of wallpapered wall. I do have pictures when the great room was being put on that show those walls in there.

Nobody really knew the room was there.

[Sally was then asked if she was able to ask Bill Raidy, after she found the room, about what she had found in the house.]

Yes, and he had no idea.

There was a pitcher and bowl on a little stand, the iron bed, nothing on the floor and a shelf that had a set of sheets for the bed; they were crisp and folded as if just from the laundry, and they were on that very primitive bookshelf. A quilt was folded on the bed.

I have the bowl, but the pitcher was cracked and broke; and the stand, it was an old iron stand, might be in the barn. We did find Civil War papers

When the Baxters started work on the basement of the Tyrell House, they discovered tin plates and candle holders resting on large stones along the walls. *Courtesy Laura Seldman.*

in the house. The kitchen was just layered with papers and everything you picked up fell apart.

The floor had a trap door leading to the cellar.

Additionally, Alice told Bill that most of the basement had been built with large heavy stones, but one small section was built with smaller stones. Mr. Raidy had not used this area, as it was sealed off from the rest of the basement for heating purposes.

As soon as it became possible, we opened the old cellar, where we discovered that the cellar at the back of the house was well constructed with mud-packed laid stone and a dirt floor. Along the walls we found many tin plates and lanterns. There appeared to be a square opening in the southeast corner that had been filled in with small stones. From the outside it was hidden by large plantings. This area appeared to be a second possible entrance and hiding place.

Not that I ever expected to find anything incredibly interesting or valuable or anything, but I knew a lot of lives had been lived in the house and that it was there in the Civil War. We think of that as being forever ago. Arrowheads from our property are in the museum here that Clarence Tyrell gave to Jean Vetter's father, Mr. Jacobs, and he gave them to the museum.

Igerna and the Ethan Perry House

Igerna was once a sizable settlement in the northern part of the Town of Chester, known as the North Gore. It is just across the Hudson River from the Town of Johnsburg. It is not known exactly where the name Igerna came from, as there is no record of any families in that area with that surname.

Houses had brick ovens, made from brick that Hanmer Meade's father, Daniel Meade, produced in his own kiln. Hanmer Meade ran a sawmill; farming and lumbering were also part of the economy. There were cider mills and a tavern, and it was a change station for stagecoaches. Three school districts operated in that area: Mead, Byrnes and Vanderwerker. Three churches served Igerna residents. The North Chester Baptist Church continues today as the Grace Bible Fellowship, and the Seventh-Day Adventist Church is still operating. The Methodist Episcopal Church, opposite the Igerna Cemetery, was torn down many years ago. There were several stores, one at Byrnes corner and one next to the Methodist Episcopal Church. A post office was established in 1889; it was closed by the post office

Ethan Perry's house was reputed to be a tavern and a stop on the Underground Railroad.
Courtesy Historical Society of the Town of Chester Archives.

department in Washington, D.C., in August 1914.[73] Today there is an Igerna road, the two surviving churches, one schoolhouse and several cemeteries that tell the names of those who lived and worked in Igerna, as well as the homes of those who call Igerna home.

One of the houses in Igerna was known locally as the Ethan Perry House. Ethan Perry was the last one in his family to live there. He lived all his life on the farm he referred to as the Reynolds Place. It came into his family when his great-grandfather Mead L. Perry married the daughter of the house, Isabella Reynolds, in 1823. Isabella was the daughter of Widow Susannah Reynolds. It is likely that the house was built for the Reynolds family, probably Susannah's in-laws. When Ethan Perry's father, Elmer, recased the front door, the name of the builder, Erastus Lake, and the date 1772 were found on the inner casing. The beams in the attic were put together with pegs. At one time it was used as a tavern and stagecoach stop on the military road from Chester to Russell. Family stories say it was also used by troops in the War of 1812. The story that the house was used as a stop on the Underground Railroad was handed down in the Perry family.

After Ethan Perry died in 1966 the house went through a succession of owners until Arthur Perryman bought it in 1997. When doing some work on

Above: Although the Perry house burned several years ago, the original barns remain intact. *Courtesy Laura Seldman.*

Below: The current owner of the Perry barns was told that Benedict Arnold stopped at the Perry tavern on his way to Montreal. *Courtesy Laura Seldman.*

Stone walls were used for pasture fences and property boundaries near the Perry house site. *Courtesy Laura Seldman.*

the house, he discovered a space under the summer kitchen, about five and a half feet high, along with an agate pitcher and a milk glass cup that was made without a handle. About eight feet from the summer kitchen there was a woodshed. In the woodshed there were a lot of old boards that had been used in the house. In the floor of the woodshed was a trapdoor to a hole in the ground. The family who lived there in the time of the Underground Railroad would have been Mead L. and Isabella Perry. Like many in the area, Mead was a farmer. Copies of some account books and other papers that were found in the house have survived in the archives of the town historian's office. Unfortunately, this house was destroyed by fire in July 2011 while it was under renovation.

Charles Fowler and the Fowler Homestead

Another merchant mentioned in Gerrit Smith's antislavery tour is Charles Fowler. He was born in Albany County, New York, on April 9, 1807. As a young man, he was one of the first traveling salesmen. He traveled into the northern part of New York, going from Albany to Chester, Schroon, Elizabethtown, Keeseville, Plattsburgh and Ogdensburg. He became acquainted with Elizabeth King Baker in Schroon, and they were married on January 10, 1832. They settled in Chester, where he was a merchant. The family first appears in Chester in the 1840 Federal Census.

Along with Joseph Leggett, Charles Fowler invested his money in land in the Chestertown area. He eventually became a wealthy man according to the standards of his time. He built a house about 1837 on Main Street in Chestertown at what he considered the halfway point on his selling route from Albany to Plattsburgh. That house is today the Chester Inn, owned by Bruce and Suzanne Robbins. It has been placed on the National Register of Historic Buildings in the Town of Chester.

Charles and Elizabeth had eight children. Two children died young. Their son Joseph, born in 1840, was a partner with his father in the general merchandise store in Chester for a while. He later moved to Glens Falls and became a manufacturer of shirts and collars in that city. He was also a director of the Glens Falls National Bank and a stockholder in many of the growing industries in Glens Falls.

Another son, Byron, born in 1845, moved to Glens Falls in 1862 and went to work as a clerk in the Glens Falls National Bank. He held that position

Charles Fowler's house was built in the 1830s and is now called the Chester Inn. *Historical Society of the Town of Chester Archives.*

The Chester Inn welcomes guests to its gracious dining room. *Courtesy Laura Seldman.*

Above: Farm tools found and housed in the original Fowler barn. *Courtesy Laura Seldman.*

Below: Fowler's barn was built against a hill and was called a "Connecticut" or "bank" barn. *Courtesy Laura Seldman.*

for about two years and then became an office manager at W.W. Rockwell, a general store in Glens Falls. With the help of his brother Joseph and the financial backing of his father, he bought out the Rockwell store and in 1869 opened Fowler's store. He became the oldest merchant of dry goods in the city of Glens Falls and the second oldest in the state. He was also a director and vice-president of the Glens Falls National Bank and was a leader in the mercantile trade.

We know that Charles Fowler was a merchant in Chester in the 1840s and was acquainted with Joseph Leggett. He is mentioned by Gerrit Smith as being sympathetic to the antislavery cause. The Fowler house was surrounded by three good-sized barns, carriage stalls and a smokehouse.

In 1999, local archaeologist David Starbuck conducted "digs" in a barn, the outhouse and the smokehouse. Some of the items that were found—buckles, clay pipes, bottles, parts of dishes and more—are displayed in the house.[74]

Although this house has not been verified as a stop on the Underground Railroad, it is not unreasonable to think that it may have been. At the very least, Charles Fowler, as a merchant in Chestertown during the Underground Railroad movement, was known to be antislavery and very likely helped provide for the fugitive slaves who passed through.

A short way south of the house, next to the Main Street Ice Cream Parlor, is a small cemetery known as the Fowler Cemetery. In that cemetery is a monument with these family names: Charles Fowler (1807–1884), Eliza K. Fowler (1810–1850), Harriet R. Fowler (second wife) (1820–1906), Jane E. Fowler (1843–1848) and Joseph Fowler (1835–1839).

Interview with Bruce Robbins Sr.

It started when we started doing the restoration work on this building. My intention was not directed toward doing this type of thing at all; it was just one thing led to another, and then the history all started just coming together. As far as the Civil War goes, I mean this house predates the Civil War in 1862. This was built in 1830, so it predates it by about thirty years. With that in mind, when you think about all the things that have transpired during the history of this house, the conversations that have taken place in this living room, you know as to what was going on around the world. We're talking, at that time, the house was built there were things that were going on in Europe and you think, "Oh my God that's ancient history," but this house was here!" Just think of the conversations. You know, not just the Civil War, there was a number of things throughout the world. I'm not going to get into all of them.

It started all coming together, when I was working on this house. I had found a number of artifacts here that all of a sudden just started making me wonder. All of a sudden I found a pair of boots behind a wall in the kitchen. And they had markings on them, and it said C.F. letters on the side of the boots. And they had all fallen apart and the stitching on them had all fallen apart. And I kinda put them together as good as I could. And, I started looking into uniforms and I come to find out they were Civil War boots. They were issued for the army. Now, why were they behind the wall? We can only suspect they were up in the attic and had gotten pushed and there was a void where they had gotten pushed to the end of the attic and they fell down behind the kitchen wall, because there was no insulation in there. That kind of led me to start thinking there's some stuff that went on here with this house.

So I started looking into some of the things that were happening during the Civil War back here in Chestertown. After working here all day on the house I'd go home and check into the history. My parents and grandparents and great-grandparents all came from this area. My great-grandfather fought in the Civil War in the 118th Adirondack Regiment under Major John L. Cunningham. This is the same Cunningham who wrote and published for his family, only a few copies of his book based on his personal war diaries titled 3 Years with the Adirondack Division. *After reading that book, I said, "You know, there's a lot of history here." Turns out Major Cunningham married Charles Fowler's daughter, and they bought a piece of property from Leggett. Cunningham's house was in back of the Leggett property. Between the Fowlers and the Leggetts, they had always had a connection, not only family-wise but property-wise. Exchanges went on for years. And we know that Leggett was the chief engineer of the UGRR in this area and was very Quaker. People were hidden in that house down there during the years of the Civil War.*

I was approached by a man a few years after we had started working on this house whose name was Mr. W. Mr. W. at that time was doing research on the UGRR for National Geographic, *and they had reason to believe that a number of places in this town were used for that. People don't understand why they would have to hide the slaves. Slaves*

Known as the "manger" in the Fowler barn, this sheltered belowground level space has been archaeologically researched in the search for evidence of fugitives' presence in the past. *Courtesy Laura Seldman.*

were a commodity, and they could have been sold back in a heartbeat. Mr. Fowler was very much against that type of thing and was very outspoken and very politically minded. Which led me to believe he couldn't have been close with the Leggetts and the Cunninghams and all that and not known about the UGRR. Mr. W. asked if he could look at the barns. He said "there are some marks here [in the manger], *we don't know, we have reason to believe they are marks that could have been done by the slaves when they came through." Since the climate is so cold up here, the manger was the place in this "bank barn"* [or Connecticut barn] *that provided a sheltered place for the horses to foal. The structure of this type of stone foundation is built on a hill. If they did have slaves down there, I think it was for short periods of time. No conclusions were made.*

This encouraged me to look around and explore further. I found a hiding place underneath the floor in the kitchen. I found another one underneath a stairway. When I opened the compartment, which was quite difficult, there were actually footprints from little kids. I had strong feelings that this house was part of the Underground Railroad. This was something that was kept secret and they wouldn't want to admit. A lot of people were not for the freeing of slaves in this area.

Then in 1999, local archaeologist David Starbuck came to take a look. Digs were conducted in the barn, the outhouse and the smokehouse. Many small artifacts were found, boxes and boxes of them: several whole bottles and many shards of glass, buckles, parts of dishes and clay pipes. Evidence showed that people were affluent. We have a shadowbox on the wall along the staircase with some of these objects.

This house was built in 1830 by Charles Fowler, and they filed the deed in 1837. Mr. Fowler was a merchant from the Albany area, originally a traveling salesman. Being the entrepreneur that he was, in the 1830s he started a wagon trade business for outlying areas beyond and between the major cities of Albany and Schenectady, selling pots and pans, knives and more. He found that if he could make a dollar on a pan in the city, he could make a dollar and a half in the outlying areas because people couldn't get those things. He eventually made enough money to buy a piece of property in Chestertown, which was pretty much between Albany and Plattsburgh. Built a two-room cabin, up and down. He bought more and more land. He became the number one merchant in the area, and very prosperous.

Current owner of the Chester Inn, Mr. Robbins, found Charles Fowler's beautifully tooled and initialed suitcase in the attic during renovations. *Courtesy Laura Seldman.*

Chestertown was considered an affluent community in the middle of everything. People of money wanted to live here. This was like a crossroads. The factory owners, not workers, lived here. There was a hat factory right across the street from the Fowler house and a glove factory where Main Street Ice Cream Parlor stands.

Mr. Fowler was also a prominent businessman in Glens Falls. He became part-owner of a company called Joint-O-Lime, selling the finest black marble. Glens Falls was an industrial center and fashion mecca. There were sewing shops above the stores.

He lived here until the 1880s. This house was always a private residence. Although after the house was sold to Mr. Downs [in the 1880s], it was known as "the cottage" and was used for VIPs

The white marble grave markers from the Fowler cemetery, found upside down and beneath several inches of soil, were first thought to be castoff slabs of stone and were considered for reuse as a new path. *Courtesy Laura Seldman.*

who came to the Chester House, which was across the street and was owned by Harry Down's father.

We bought the house in 1987, worked on it for two years and opened it as the Chester Inn in 1989. Then it took three more years to complete the work. At the time of purchase, they had already had an auction that had cleared out the contents. We did find a suitcase with the initials CF in the attic.

[Bruce was asked how he found the gravestones that were in the barn.] *We were doing some work around the outside of the barns, shoring up the stone pillars, while we were pulling the dirt away and we noticed these white marble slabs. We intended to use them as walkways until we turned them over and revealed the names.*

6

TOWN OF CHESTER ABOLITIONISTS

*T*here were those in town who were connected to the Underground Railroad movement. Although they were not owners of an Underground Railroad site, they were sympathetic to the cause and aided it in other ways.

Ezra B. Smith

Ezra B. Smith was born on October 15, 1794, the son of Abijah and Keziah Botsford Smith. He married Laura, and they had daughters Catherine and Caroline. Catherine died in 1843 at age seventeen. Caroline married Charles H. Faxon of Chester. Ezra owned and operated a general store on the lot just north of the Presbyterian church in Chestertown in the 1830s and 1840s. In the 1840s Charles Faxon joined the business, Smith & Faxon. He is mentioned in Gerrit Smith's 1845 antislavery tour as one of the merchants in Chester "whose intelligence and integrity will not permit them to remain longer in their pro-slavery connections." In the Federal Census records of 1840 and 1850, he is listed as a farmer and then a merchant. Smith was active in the Presbyterian Church from its beginnings, being one of the first elders.[75] Ezra died on March 15, 1881, and his wife, Laura, died on January 20, 1863. They were first interred in the Village Cemetery on Theriot Avenue and were removed from there in 1883 and placed on the Smith-Faxon lot in Chester Rural Cemetery.

Nathan and James W. Tubbs

Mr. Tubbs is another merchant mentioned in Gerrit Smith's antislavery tour. The records show that Nathan and James Tubbs owned and ran a store in the 1840s in Chestertown. That puts them in the town as merchants during Gerrit Smith's antislavery tour in 1845. They were sympathetic to the antislavery cause; perhaps Smith thought they could be counted on to provide help and provisions for the escaping slaves traveling through the Town of Chester.

In the archives of the Town of Chester Historian's office is a justice docket for the years 1846–50. It contains many court cases involving Nathan and J.W. Tubbs as they sought to collect on monies owed them for goods, wares and merchandise. Deeds show that Nathan and James purchased land in Chester as early as 1839. Nathan Tubbs and his wife, Clarissa, appear in the 1850 Federal Census in Chestertown. The Tubbs name does not appear in the census records after that. The last appearance of Nathan or James W. Tubbs in the assessment records is in 1851.

William Hotchkiss

William Hotchkiss first appears in the Town of Chester when he is appointed postmaster on September 5, 1834. He went on to be appointed again in 1844, 1851 and 1857. He is listed in the 1840 Federal Census with an adult female, most likely his wife, Elizabeth, and five children.

Hotchkiss was born in the city of Albany, New York, on August 21, 1806. His wife, Elizabeth Sherman, was born in Coeymans, Albany County, on April 24, 1806. They were married in 1827 in Albany. William and Elizabeth, with their two oldest children, left Albany and came to Chester in December 1831. Four more children were born to them in Chester.

His name appears as an elder in the First Presbyterian Church in Chestertown in 1843. In a letter in the April 22, 1846 issue of the *Glens Falls Republican*, William Hotchkiss of Chestertown promised to "vote to abolish the property qualification" in the cause of full Negro suffrage. In 1846 William was elected as a delegate to the Constitutional Convention to revise the Constitution of the State of New York.

The 1850 Federal Census lists William's occupation as tailor. Perhaps it is in that capacity that he helped to aid the fugitive slaves who came through the town. He was also very involved in town politics. He was supervisor of the Town of Chester on four different occasions (1838, 1843–45, 1853 and 1860). This means he was town supervisor at the times Abel Brown and Gerrit Smith stopped in Chestertown to give antislavery speeches. For the 1856–57 term, he was elected senator of the Fourteenth Senatorial District, which comprised the counties of Warren, Essex and Clinton. In 1859 he was appointed executive clerk in the Senate and again in 1862 and 1863. He does not appear in the Town of Chester after the 1860 Federal Census. From 1863 until 1868, William was appointed assistant chief of the Bureau of Military Statistics, located in the city of Albany. That department was abolished in 1868. At that time William and Elizabeth moved to Glens Falls, and he was elected to the office of the justice of the peace from 1869 to 1873.[76] In April 1869 William Hotchkiss was appointed deputy collector of the First Division, Sixteenth District, Internal Revenue. That is the position he held at the time he wrote a short biography of his life to that point, about 1870. A copy of that biography is in the archives of the Town of Chester Historian's office. William and Elizabeth are in Queensbury in the 1870 Federal Census, where William's occupation is listed as "Dept. U.S. Colls."

William Hotchkiss died on April 30, 1880. Elizabeth died on June 25, 1883. They are both buried at Glens Falls Cemetery, Glens Falls, New York.

Dr. Morgan Pritchard

Morgan W. Pritchard was the son of Richard and May Jeffers Pritchard. He was born on June 3, 1799, in Carmarthenshire, Wales. His family immigrated to America before March 1802. In 1802 the family is found in Chester, Warren County. Morgan was naturalized as a citizen in Warren County on September 11, 1822. He was certified to teach school in December 1818; he was then nineteen years old. He studied medicine at the Vermont Academy of Medicine and received certificates in the study of medicine in 1824, 1825 and 1827. On February 23, 1827, Morgan W. Pritchard was granted "the Privilege of practicing Physic and Surgery" in New York State by the Medical Society of the County of Warren.[77]

Dr. Pritchard was mentioned in Gerrit Smith's journal of his 1845 antislavery tour as being one of the "abolitionists of the truest class."

Pritchard bought a house in Chestertown in 1844 and, according to census records, resided in Chestertown until at least 1870. The house that once belonged to Dr. Morgan Pritchard is now the office of the Upstate Insurance Company.

Pritchard died in Horicon in 1877. He and his wife, Lydia, are buried at the Darrowsville Cemetery in the Town of Chester.

Myron Tripp

Myron Tripp was born on January 4, 1818, in Warrensburgh, New York, the son of Nathaniel and Jane Tripp. He married Eliza Jeffers in Luzerne in 1844.

On July 14, 1843, he helped organize the Wesleyan Methodist Church at Darrowsville. It was known as the Warrensburgh-Darrowsville Church. He was active in the church, at times attending the yearly conference of the Wesleyan Methodist Church in Syracuse, and was a member at the time of his death.[78]

In 1864 Myron and Charles Loy established a hardware store in Chestertown called Tripp & Loy. This building was the site of the former Ezra B. Smith store. Myron and Eliza had two daughters; Adeliza was born in October 1846 and married Charles Loy, her father's partner, on March 31, 1871; Eunice was born in 1850 and died on January 26, 1871. Tripp & Loy operated their hardware business until 1880, when it became J.R. Dunn and Company.

Myron's sister, Jane Ann Tripp, married Reverend S.H. Foster, an abolitionist minister who was very active in the Underground Railroad movement. He served the Darrowsville Wesleyan Methodist Church (1864–70, 1879–81 and 1893–94). His brother Joseph became a minister and served the Darrowsville Wesleyan Methodist Church in the 1880s.

Myron Tripp's obituary identifies him as a "highly respected resident of Chester." He was prominently identified with the church and charitable works in the town. He died on March 28, 1897. His first wife, Eliza, died on December 6, 1885. They are buried at the Chester Rural Cemetery.

Reverend Andrew D. Milne

Andrew D. Milne was born in 1808 in Scotland. He was the son of John and Janet Duncan Milne. Elder A.D. Milne came to Chester in May 1851 as pastor of the Baptist church in Chestertown. He was the tenth pastor and served Minerva and Bolton as well. The church stood where the Main Street Ice Cream Parlor is today. The building was erected in 1818, moved once and remodeled once. He "was of Scotch descent and possessed more than ordinary ability as an effective author, preacher, and writer." In 1855 he published a Baptist monthly called the *Star of Destiny*. He was also the author of a temperance allegory, *Uncle Sam's Farm Fence*, for the Baptist Association.[79] The 1855 New York State Census places him in Chester with his wife, Ann, and sons William O. and Joseph S. Milne. At that time they had been in Chester for four years. On that census his occupation is clergyman.

He left the ministry in 1855 and purchased the offices of the short-lived *Warren County Whig*, a Glens Falls publication that had begun in 1855. On January 2, 1856, he published the first issue of the *Glens Falls Messenger*, a small, two-page paper. It mostly comprised stories and advertisements for medicines and merchandise. The first issue had an antislavery sketch, written by Milne, on the front page.

According to the 1885 *History of Warren County*, edited by H.P. Smith, Milne "was an easy and vigorous writer" and started the *Messenger* as a paper "devoted to subjects of a moral and religious character, with the intention of having nothing to do with politics except so far as they may have a direct bearing upon the destinies of the great brotherhood of man." Milne was a strong temperance and antislavery advocate, and this was reflected in his writings. Due to this, the paper naturally drifted in the support of the Republican nominee for president, John C. Frémont. From that time on, the *Messenger* was a Republican paper.

Andrew Milne was also an inventor and, after starting the *Glens Falls Messenger*, invented Milne's Electro Anti-Corrosive Ink. A letter from a satisfied customer in the July 23, 1857 issue of the *Glens Falls Messenger* says the ink "preserves the pen and at the same time flows so easily," "does not corrode in pen" and "flows freely."

In the April 8, 1858 edition Mr. Milne stated that "feeble health has admonished us for some time that our labors as a publisher and editor must cease." L.A. Arnold then acted as editor and Norman Cole as publisher. In 1863 Arnold purchased Norman's interest and became both editor and publisher. The paper continued until 1890.

In 1866 Andrew D. Milne died in Fall River, Massachusetts, age fifty-eight. In his death record his occupation was listed as writer and clergyman. He is buried at Oak Grove Cemetery in Fall River. In the same cemetery we find his parents, John Milne (1775–1857) and Janette Duncan Milne (died June 3, 1838); his wife, Anna Tennant Dunlap (1817–95); and his sons, Lieutenant Joseph S. Milne (died July 7, 1863, at Gettysburg) and William O. Milne (died June 16, 1912). Anna married Timothy Dunlap after Andrew Milne died.

Reverend S.H. Foster

Solomon H. Foster was the youngest member to be ordained in the Wesleyan Methodist Church shortly after the Utica convention was called. The Wesleyan Church was organized, and the antislavery struggle began. According to a short remembrance in the October 20, 1898 edition of the *Ticonderoga Sentinel*, Reverend Foster became "one of the foremost anti-slavery agitators beginning in early manhood and earnestly working for the cause until victory came." He was one of the best-known ministers in northern New York, having preached in Warren, Essex, Clinton, Franklin and St. Lawrence Counties. He also preached in Syracuse, Watertown, Rome and Ontario. He was an able preacher and deeply spiritual and was beloved as pastor and a friend.[80] Reverend Foster served churches in Hague, Potsdam, Keeseville, Ellenburg, West Chazy and Weybridge, Vermont, as well as the Darrowsville Wesleyan Methodist Church in Chester. He was one of the ministers in charge of the organization of the Wesleyan Methodist Church in Hadley in 1844. He was the Wesleyan Methodist Champlain Conference president (district superintendent) in 1863, 1864 and 1870.[81] On the occasion of Jane A. Foster's death, it was requested that the *Warrensburgh News* publish her obituary from the September 7 issue of the *Wesleyan Methodist*. That obituary appeared in the October 6, 1904 issue of the *Warrensburgh News*. Her obituary quotes from a letter from one of her sons: "When young she united with the Methodist Episcopal Church, and it was as a boy preacher that she became acquainted with my father and they were married Nov. 19, 1840, the day he was twenty years of age. Shortly after the Utica convention was called, my father was the youngest member and was ordained at that time."

Solomon and Jane Foster had five children, the first three dying at young ages from diphtheria. The other two were Gardner and Matt Foster. Gardner became a medical doctor. He was a specialist for fourteen years in ear, nose and throat diseases at Rochester and was a member of many medical and other societies. He passed away on December 10, 1914, at Schenectady at the age of sixty-five.

Mattlock Foster was born about 1854 in West Chazy, New York. He died on September 5, 1933, at Schenectady. In 1897 he married Julie Elizabeth Oliver in Philadelphia. She later became known as Jeanne Robert Foster, a well-known author and friend of John Butler Yeats, the Irish portrait painter. Yeats is buried in the Foster family plot in the Chester Rural Cemetery.

In a 1962 letter written to a resident of Chestertown, Jeanne Robert Foster says this about her father-in-law: "Becoming a clergyman at such an early age, he was called the 'boy preacher' of the Wesleyan Methodist Church. He had attended the famous Syracuse Conference where the abolitionists split off from the M.E. Church and founded the Wesleyan Methodist Church opposed to slavery and to oathbound secret societies." She went on to say that "Father Foster, who died when I was a little girl, looked like Henry Ward Beecher and—even in old age—had a magnificent voice and preached magnetically."

Census records and his death record tell us that Solomon H. Foster was born in Ohio in 1820. His parents are unknown. He died on June 8, 1893, at Chestertown. He married Jane Ann Tripp on November 19, 1840. She died on July 28, 1904, at Chestertown. Jane was the daughter of Nathaniel Tripp and Jane Place Tripp and the sister of Myron Tripp, one of the founders of the Darrowsville Wesleyan Methodist Church. They are both buried at Chester Rural Cemetery in Chestertown.

7.

TWO NEW SITES

Warrensburg: Interview with LouAnn Springer

In the mid-nineteenth century, Ms. Springer's great-great-grandfather Griffin built two houses on River Street just below the bridge over the Schroon River at Library Avenue. Ms. Springer's house has been described as a side-gabled, wood-framed cottage.

Several years ago, Ms. Springer and her brother had to take down part of the house (in the rear, on the river side). They found the "entrance" to an underneath section, supported by two large stones on each side; some scraps of metal covered the opening. Inside were a couple of large wooden shelves, extra wide and far apart. They also found an indoor outhouse/privy in that area. Surprisingly, this is where they found her grandmother's silver!

Still clearly visible at the edge of the river fifteen feet above the riverbed is the stone foundation for the livery, also built and run by Griffin, with stone steps up to it from the water's edge.

Ms. Springer recalled that when she was a young child, she found an old trunk filled with very old clothes here on the landing at the base of the foundation.

The story of hiding the slaves was told in the family. They definitely used the Schroon River. Ms. Springer said her family thought it was the right thing to do.

Above: Springer family stories identify their house on the Schroon River in Warrensburg as an Underground Railroad site. *Courtesy Laura Seldman.*

Above and opposite, bottom: Behind the house, the remains of the foundation for the livery are clearly visible fifteen to twenty feet above the Schroon River bank. *Courtesy Laura Seldman.*

Ms. Springer added that some years ago (early 1980s) she spoke to Leah, the daughter of Warrensburg dentist Dr. Speidel. They believed their house, known as Dr. Howard's house on Main Street, was also on the UGRR. She recalled the story that they used to hang a quilt from the porch; different colors had different meanings.

Ms. Springer was told by Leah, the daughter of town dentist Dr. Speidel, that their house was part of the UGRR. *Courtesy Laura Seldman.*

Following pages: In the 1800s, there was a boat landing at the southern end of Schroon Lake, serving water travel to the north. *Courtesy Laura Seldman.*

Schroon Lake:
Interview with Laura and Wayne Dewey

UGRR historian Don Papson shared an e-mail he had received from the historian in North Hudson–Schroon Lake, Laura Dewey. We were all searching for details of connections between stations and conductors in this region north of Albany and up to Canada.

At our meeting in Schroon Lake a year later in August 2015, Ms. Dewey showed us an article that was from a special 2004 bicentennial edition of the *Ticonderoga Sentinel* in their historical society archives, which reproduced a copy of the *Schroon Lake Star* from July 1906.

An Underground Railroad Stop

During the 1850s a section of the famous Underground Railroad went through Schroon Lake Village and adjoining towns. John Brown and many helping hands made it possible for escaping slaves to find freedom in Canada, aided by some of our local citizens. The slaves were told to follow the North Star as a guide. Their frustrated owners, amazed by the number of escapes, said to themselves, "They must have taken an underground railroad" to elude capture. Hence the name.

Today, at the intersection of Route 9 and Route 73 [should be Route 74] *still stands the Platt house, now the home of Louise and Chester Hargreaves. (Louise was born there.) The fleeing negroes were picked up at the Leggetts' home in Chestertown by Dan Platt and Ransom Seaman and brought to the house to wait until men from Elizabethtown picked them up and sent them on their way to the border.*

The White Lodge in Schroon Lake. *Courtesy Wayne and Laura Dewey, North Hudson and Schroon Lake Historical Society.*

Who Were Platt and Seaman?

Looking at the 1858 *Beers Atlas* land records, Dewey found that these men were neighbors living just one house away. Both had originally come from Lanesboro, Massachusetts.

The house Daniel Platt built in 1810 and where he first lived became known as the White Lodge. His son James Platt later built Carisbrooke on the neighboring hill and lived there.

Louise Hargreaves had a personal connection to Platt. Her father worked for Platt as a young man and later as caretaker of Carisbrooke. She and her husband, Chester, managed the White Lodge (and Carisbrooke) as summer guesthouses for the Platt family.

Hargreaves became historian of Schroon. Her handwritten personal journal (sixteen notebooks) has been organized by Paul Stapley, a later historian of Schroon Lake, as a short story, "Life at our Farm House."

From page 104 in Louise Hargreaves's notebook, in her own handwriting:

> *Dan Platt (father of these men) strongly sympathized with the slaves. He and Ransom Seaman over the hill used to harbor the runaway slaves. These men went to Chestertown brot back Negroes. Kept them til a propitious time came to get them on north to Canada and freedom.*

Nancy Dillon of Schroon Lake acknowledges Louise Hargreaves as the source of information for an article entitled "As I Saw It," a first-person account from the daughter-in-law of Daniel Platt, Alice:

> *Many stories are told of Carisbrooke some true, some untrue. But, it is true that the old white house, where Hargreaves now lives, and too, the one owned by Ransom Seamons, were used to harbor run-away slaves. Dan strongly sympathized with the slaves. The slaves were brought up from Chestertown in some kind of closed carriage. They were kept right at the house with the family. There was very rarely any need to hide them. The Negroes stayed there until a proper time, when they were sent north toward Canada.*

As even further confirmation, Ms. Dewey found a notation in the margin of a letter from Paul Shapley to Louise Hargreaves in the town hall archives:

> *"William Wessels, Adirondack profiles, p.55."*
> *Here (Schroon Lake) also was the home of Dan Platt which was a station on the UGRR to Canada prior to the Civil War which home is now the lovely residence of Mrs. Louise Hargreaves.*

Above: Revealed! The hiding place for fugitives was beneath one end of the front porch and was apparently connected by a door to the basement. *Courtesy Chloe Seldman.*

Opposite: The harsh winter of 2015 destroyed much of what was left of the already deteriorating structure, including the front porch. *Courtesy Laura Seldman.*

Mr. Wessels owned the Blue Mountain House (became the Adirondack Museum) and was the founder of the first Adirondack Historical Society. This small publication from 1960 contains primary source material from local town historians.[82]

In August 2015, the Deweys (Laura, with husband historian, Wayne) took us to visit the once-majestic White Lodge. We had mixed feelings knowing its history, seeing it in ruins but grateful to see the remains before the bulldozer buried it entirely. Its demise in the mid-1960s was assured as the Northway was built just out the back door.

At this visit, having seen this property over a period of several years, Dewey noticed that the effects of the previous rough and snowy winter weather had destroyed the roof and more. The front porch boards had rotted through and fallen in, revealing a small room (four and a half feet by nine feet)! The space below was lined with stones with a closed door to the rest of the cellar. The rest of the area under the porch was a shallow space (less than a foot deep). This was most probably the hiding space.

8.

MATERIAL CULTURE

*T*he process of extensive investigation of possible Town of Chester safe house sites led to the discovery of another subject for study: objects of interest. Examining artifacts with full descriptions can help place them in history. Although they are not necessarily connected to the UGRR, they inform what remains of pieces from mid-nineteenth-century Adirondack life, describing material culture in the Town of Chester.

The National Museum of American History has a collection of more than three million different artifacts. They are permanent records of our past and reflect how people lived day to day. Artifacts make history feel more real.[83]

While artifacts may not tell us specific information, it is because of where they were found that they are significant. Analyzing material evidence is like writing an object's biography. There is a story for each object, including the people who made and used it. When historians analyze material objects, they begin by recording basic information—a written or verbal description, measurements and photographs. Next, dating the object and determining who owned and used it supply useful details.

"Objects," write Appleby, Hunt and Jacob, "arouse curiosity, resist implausible manipulation, and collect layers of information about them."[84]

Material culture supports a broader understanding of what a site was and of the life of the people who acted there.[85]

Quilts

When we found nine quilts at two "safe houses," we realized that these items needed to be carefully examined by quilt experts. What was the significance of these quilts? Ultimately, we discovered that there is no evidence that any of these quilts were connected to the UGRR.

Nevertheless, this is a true story. At the evening gathering of the Historical Society of the Town of Chester in August 2013, the educator and guest speaker from Moreau recounted plausible stories about quilts as codes as part of the UGRR. He believed quilts were used to communicate, based on patterns and colors, sometimes using double-sided quilts. He had with him quilt reproductions of patterns familiar to many: Log Cabin, Evening Star and Flying Geese.

According to quilt professional Miller, this lecture is considered to be "the legend we would love to believe." There is no evidence to support this. Unfortunately it is sometimes still taught to schoolchildren as part of their history curriculum.

Noted quilt historians have all weighed in:

> *We have no historical evidence of quilts being used as signals, codes or maps.* (**Barbara Brackman**)[86]

> *To many of us the use of quilts as messengers on the UGRR is a myth. It cannot be proven through recorded historical documents or defendable oral history.* (**Kimberly Wulfert**)[87]

> *The idea of quilts being used in the Underground Railroad for purposes other than bedding was not mentioned either in the written documents of the period or in the interviews given years later.* (**Kris Driessen**)[88]

Where Did This Quilt Code Story Come From?

Probably the earliest mention of a quilt code appeared in the late 1980s in a short statement that was made in a video: quilts were hung outside UGRR safe houses (no reference for that assertion was given). Historian Leigh Fellner notes that this period coincided with the post-bicentennial revival of folk art, the popularization of women's history studies and the emergence of African culture stereotypes.[89]

Stitched from the Soul (1989) by Gladys-Marie Fry introduced evidence of slave-made quilts to early quilting history. Deborah Hopkinson was inspired by a discussion of the symbolism in these quilts to write a fictional story, *Sweet Clara and the Freedom Quilt* (1993), indicating that a quilt may have been used as a signaling device in the UGRR.

Hidden in Plain View (1999), written by Jacqueline Tobin and Raymond Dobard, claimed that handmade pieced quilts were actually codes used for traveling along the UGRR. The book claimed to document discussions with Ozella McDaniel Williams, who told of a quilt code related to the quilt block names, shapes and colors and the counted knots that hid messages for escaping slaves. The authors later admitted to mixing truth with conjecture.

Prominent African American historian Giles Wright clearly debunked this story in an essay and presentation for the New Jersey Historical Association in 2001, citing incorrect details and lack of verification or corroborating resources.

Further exploiting the proliferation of historical fiction, author Jennifer Chiaverini writes novels that interweave history and imagination, including the popular Elm Creek Quilt series. In particular, *The Sugar Camp Quilt* narrates an adventure of one family's dedicated involvement in aiding runaway slaves using a quilt as a safe house signal and possibly as a station guide.

By humanizing the story, we are made to feel it is true.

Bestselling writer Sue Monk Kidd, in her book *Invention of Wings* (2014), based her fiction on real people, the highly regarded abolitionist sisters Angelina and Sarah Grimke. However, the quilt in this story is not given a mythical role. It tells one slave's personal story, as it is part of the material culture of the period.

By involving details of authentic historical figures, we are made to feel the story is true. It confuses the actual historical facts.

We can only say that there is no evidence that any of the quilts we uncovered were used as signals or code, but they do represent an interesting slice of history, a real piece of the material culture from a certain location and from the same family. These quilts were made most likely by multiple generations covering at least half a century.

There are methods for determining the age of a quilt. Author and quilter Barbara Brackman has mastered the details of fabrics, their history and the creative ways the past and the present can connect through quilting: stitching and piecing. Her books provide invaluable resources, including a reproducible worksheet for identifying and dating antique quilts.[90]

Brackman devised a system for categorizing and dating quilts, looking at clues as bits of evidence for figuring out a range of years. If citing "circa" 1850, it implies a ten-year span on either side of the date.

The newest textile in the group will give you a starting date.
The two most important clues are fabric and style, defined as borders and set (the way the quilt is organized).
Other clues are color, techniques (pieced or appliqued and quilting types) and patterns.
Measuring the space between quilting lines can tell you a great deal about when the quilt was made, as will the number of stitches per inch and the pattern of quilting lines.
Lack of machine sewing supports a date of before 1840.
Tied quilts almost always date from after 1875.
The last clue is the most obvious: inscriptions, names, etc.

Leggett Quilts

We were most fortunate to have quilt professionals from New York State—Lynne Bennett, Debra Grana, Sharon Waddell and Linda Miller—examine our nine quilts.

The yellow Leggett quilt looked remarkably similar to the well-known crib quilt by Lydia Maria Child that is now at the Historic New England Museum. They are similar to the untrained eye but actually use different patterns. The yellow star quilt (known as a Sawtooth or Evening Star) has fabrics that indicate a range of years. The red with tan and blue star fabric indicate 1850s, but the added red/black checks say later. The striped madder with paisley and chocolate browns hint at the 1860s. The on-point set and alternate plain blocks say even earlier. Yet the lack of border, green/blue gingham check stars and the sparse, grid quilting indicate a later date. This quilt dates to the mid-nineteenth century, circa 1850–65. The yellow calico was very popular for children's dresses.

The pink and green quilt is known as an Ohio Star. Judging by the fabrics in it, it dates to 1850. The quilt professionals thought this quilt was very likely made by the same person as the first quilt. It is a star (though Ohio Star pattern this time), set on point, with alternating blocks of printed fabric, no border and simple outline quilting around the stars and grid/line quilting elsewhere. The star fabrics are earlier (1850s to 1860s). The over-dyed green

Evening Star Leggett quilt. *Courtesy Laura Seldman.*

has more yellow tone than blue, which is typical of the earlier greens. (Later greens tended to be more blue than yellow.) This quilt was likely made in the late quarter of the 1800s, but earlier than the previous quilt.

There are two similar red and white quilts. One is noticeably more worn than the other. A variation of Mariner's Compass, the print design looks to be circa 1840. It comes closest to No. 3661, Grandma's Favorite Compass or Setting Sun on page 439 of Brackman's *Encyclopedia of Pieced Quilted Patterns*.[91] The red fabric has some of the bubble seaweed motifs that were popular in early 1800s, according to Meller and Elffers.[92] Similar fabrics are also dated to pre-1830, plus 1830–60 in Trestain.[93] The fabric could be from the first quarter of the 1800s, but the block style of the quilt is a bit later, so the date would be circa 1850.

The red and white quilt in better condition, Mariner's Compass, has fabrics that are not as distinctive. Judging by the Turkey Red, the pieced pattern and the density of the quilting, this would be circa 1840–60. The block in this quilt is called chips and whetstones (a variation of the Mariner's

Above: Ohio Star Leggett quilt. *Courtesy Laura Seldman.*

Below: Older variation of Mariner's Compass Leggett quilt. *Courtesy Laura Seldman.*

Left: Another variation of Mariner's Compass, Chips and Whetstones Leggett quilt. *Courtesy Laura Seldman.*

Below: Checkerboard Leggett quilt. *Courtesy Laura Seldman.*

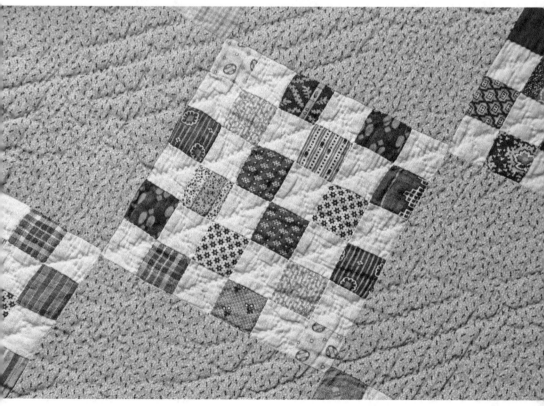

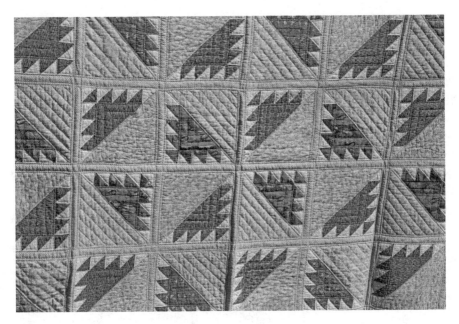

Lost Ship Leggett quilt. *Courtesy Laura Seldman.*

Compass). This pattern is very old, theoretically based on the sailor compass rose. The red/white color scheme was first popular starting in the 1840s. The fancy quilting (rather than the straight line or grid quilting of the other two) tends to be from the 1840s to 1870s, or later, if the quilt maker just liked to quilt. Overall, this one would date to circa 1850.

The one with the checkerboard pattern is circa 1850s to 1860s. It has distinctive madder prints, and the orange print was popular for children's wear. The checkerboard design quilt looks hardly used. It is a type of sampler quilt, from circa 1865.

The Lost Ship quilt also looks minimally used. This quilt has typical madder printed calicos dated circa 1860. The fabrics overlap with other quilts. The quilting is similar, with grids and lines.

The quilted coverlet with the uneven nine patch is not as early as the others. Whoever did this was not a quilter or a sewer. Fabric used with the claret dye was made only in 1890–1910. This quilt would date to circa 1900.

This family collection is probably the work of several quilters, perhaps from different generations. But they also show that they were not done at a quilting bee, where different "sewing hands" would be noticeable.

The Tyrell Quilt

The patchwork double-sided quilt was found in the home of the Baxters.

Quilt professionals see the large piece of cadet blue fabric as a date indicator—1870s. One quilt expert noted the "lumpy bumpy" batting in one section, some machine stitching, and discovered another older quilt inside. Noticeable on the Giant Log Cabin side are mourning prints, from when Queen Victoria was mourning the death of her husband, Prince Albert (1861), dating this quilt closer to the last quarter of the nineteenth century. The two sides were tied separately.

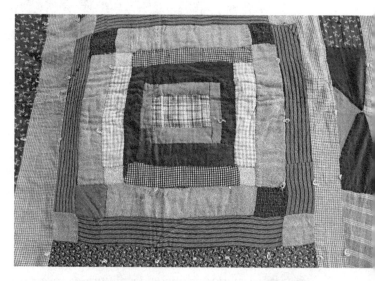

Top: On the Lob Cabin side of the Tyrell quilt, owner Sally Baxter pointed out the noticeably different fabric piece in the southeast corner of the central rectangle, marking the location of the hidden room. *Courtesy Laura Seldman.*

Right: Side two of the Tyrell quilt is a distinctly different, brightly colored patchwork. *Courtesy Laura Seldman.*

Shoes

While shoes don't tell us specific information about the Underground Railroad, they can provide insight about fugitives' needs. When slaves ran away, if they had been field workers, they may not have had any shoes. If they had been house workers, they may have had shoes, but perhaps not a pair that would sustain the long journey to freedom. Slave shoes were easily recognizable. In this way shoes have come to symbolize the freedom seeker's journey.[94]

Shoes and shoe forms have been found in the attics of several known or suspected Underground Railroad sites (at the Tripp and Temperance Tavern sites and in homes in the Capital District of the Albany area). It is likely they were placed there after the journey was over as an invocation of good luck and prosperity and to ensure the success of the household.

Top: Hand-carved wooden shoe forms for men, women and children were discovered in different areas of the Tripp house. *Courtesy Laura Seldman.*

Bottom: On the windowsill at the Leggetts' rests an early Paul Revere punched tin lantern. It was commonly carried from place to place, lighting the subject only, not the whole room. *Courtesy Laura Seldman.*

Paul Revere Lantern

Paul Revere lanterns, also known as punched tin lanterns, are true lanterns and not "candle carriers." Instead of removing the candle upon arrival at its destination, the candle would be left inside and the lantern door would be opened. At the time they were originally made, 1780 to 1840, the custom was to light the task and not the room, so the tin-coated back and sides of the lantern are intended to reflect and concentrate the candlelight in a primitive form of beam, while continuing to protect the candle from blowing out. A pre–Civil War barn was full of combustible materials; using an exposed candle would have been quite risky. By keeping the candle inside the lantern with the lantern door open, an adequate amount of illumination would be produced while the risk of fire was significantly reduced. The candle heat from a "short six" (size) does collect in the cone-shaped hood, but diminishes significantly about mid-lantern. The natural draft created by the many openings tends to cool things down.

Rope Beds

Rope beds needed regular tightening, done with a special tool called a bed key or straining wrench. Mr. S found this handmade key in the Tripp house. *Courtesy Laura Seldman.*

Early beds were not held together securely. Long tenons on the rails were fitted into deep mortises in the posts, and the rope spring held everything together. All was well until the rope stretched and slackened, and then the entire bed became wobbly until the rope was re-tightened.

A bed rope needed to be forty to one hundred feet long, depending on the width and length of the bed and the number of holes in the sides of the frame. To assemble these beds was a project requiring several people to hold the parts in place while one strung and tightened the rope with a wooden straining wrench. This wrench, also known as a rope key, bed key or rope wrench, resembles an oversized clothespin with a crossbar through it for additional leverage.[95]

Rope began to be replaced by metal spring mattresses after 1840.[96] Modern legend has it that the phrase "sleep tight" comes from rope beds being more comfortable when the ropes are tight.[97]

9.

ARCHAEOLOGY

*O*nly in the last four decades have researchers devoted much attention to the African American component of sites, both in the North and the South.

"For a long time, archaeologists who studied plantations were mostly interested in the people who lived in the big house," said Syracuse University anthropologist Theresa Singleton. "That didn't tell us much more about slaves than we learned from the histories by the people who enslaved them. Archaeology allows us to see history through a different lens."[98]

In the 1960s, the rise of the civil rights movement and the push for African American studies programs in universities caused historical archaeologists to reevaluate their perspective.

Because the written record of slavery from the slaves' point of view is so meager, archaeology—with its emphasis on the physical landscape and material aspects of culture—is emerging as an important means of filling in omissions and distortions.[99]

"Written history is always subject to a kind of cultural amnesia. Some of it is deliberately forgotten and some of it is inadvertently lost. That's why artifacts and their context are so important. They can speak to us for the people who left no written record."[100]

By the 1980s, African American archaeology had become an established and respected subdiscipline of historical archaeology with its own journals, symposiums, newsletters and meetings. It was initially called "Slave Archaeology" but is now more frequently referred to as "Early African-American Archaeology."

There is some evidence that pipes found on plantations in border states were part of the material culture of slave populations.[101]

In the Town of Chester only one site has been professionally excavated. At the Chester Inn, the former Fowler property, well-known local archaeologist David Starbuck enlisted local residents to assist in the dig. They found sherds of pottery and many pieces of clay pipes.

At the Tripp property, cellar holes (remnants of early log cabins) were dug and examined by the owners. They reported finding similar items and all sorts of glass bottles.

Potteries

Fort Edward was one of the nation's major centers for production of stoneware in the latter part of the nineteenth century. Along with Sandy Hill, the town was ideal for this industry because of its proximity to the Hudson River (both were on the east bank), to the Champlain Canal and to

Commonly found, pieces of ceramic stoneware from the mid-1800s are called "sherds." The sherd found at the Leggetts' is from a five-gallon crock. *Courtesy Laura Seldman.*

railways and highways and the availability of earthen clay, wood for burning in the kilns and cheap waterpower.[102]

Potteries were first built there in 1858; at one point there were five in these two towns. By 1941 they had all closed. Feldspar, an ingredient needed for stoneware production, could have been supplied by the mine in Darrowsville forty-five miles away.

American stoneware was largely produced as utilitarian ware to be used in the home and for everyday life. Ovoid forms were earliest. Later straight-edged forms often had an intense cobalt decoration under a salt glaze.[103]

Salt firing and salt glazing have been common practice in ceramics for centuries, initially as an industrial glazing method and then as an artistic treatment and technique in studio ceramics. The salt is inserted into the heated kiln, and the salt vaporizes (turns into a gas) and adheres to the clay body of the pottery, making a glaze. Not only does salt glazing seal the ware, but it also creates a distinctive orange-peel texture that has become a desirable decorative trait of salt-glazed ware.[104]

Pipes

White clay pipes were found at both locations where digs were made in the Town of Chester. These tobacco pipes from England were similar to those found by the thousands at Colonial Williamsburg. The size of the pipe bowl was increased over time to keep up with fashion and to allow more tobacco to be consumed. Long pipe stems allowed a cooler smoke but also broke more easily.

Archaeologists have evolved a specific method for dating pipe stems that shows a relationship between size of bore (pipe stem opening) and the year they were made (later was smaller).

According to J.C. Harrington's initial studies in the 1950s, the time periods and average bore diameters show that from 1590 to 1620 the bore was 9/64 and, from 1680 to 1720, the bore was only 4/64, indicating that the later the period, the smaller the bore.[105] This change in diameter may have occurred because pipe stems became longer through time, requiring a smaller bore. The pipes were most often cleaned by being set on a rack and placed overnight in a fireplace.

Historian J. Speight considers slave-made clay pipes found on plantations from slave sites in Virginia and Maryland to be the first form of African

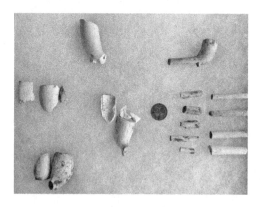

Mr. S collected white clay pipes from his own excavations on the Tripp property. *Courtesy Mr. S.*

American folk art. The pipes were all made by hand between 1640 and 1740—the period when the largest numbers of enslaved Africans were imported to work the tobacco plantations throughout the Chesapeake Bay area. These pipes were red or rust colored because they were fired in an open fire. They often had incised designs that appeared African—in fact, most similar to Mali in western Africa. These pipes seem to disappear around 1740, considerably earlier than our period of investigation.[106]

Glass Bottles

Before 1814 glass bottles were hand-blown in England and France, many with identifying characteristics. After that, most bottles were formed by blowing molten glass into a mold. Molds were made of iron or wood in standard sizes and shapes. When the bottle was removed from a mold, a faint seam remained in the glass, running from the base to a point somewhere between the shoulder up to the top edge of the mouth. In a general way, the height of the mold seam on the bottle can indicate age—that is, the higher the seam goes, the newer the bottle.[107]

Lips were applied separately until 1903, when the process was mechanized. The hot glass was applied to the neck and then hand-tooled to the proper shape. Different lip shapes related to date periods—that is, flared lips (1830–50), rolled lips (1840–60), sheared lips (1830–50) and applied blob lips (1840–70). This was done crudely before 1880, when a lipping tool was used for uniform shape. This process erased the mold seam and left telltale concentric rings on the lip. Dating was aided by noticing the "pontil" on the bottom, a mark left where the bottle detached from the "punty" rod, which held the bottle as the lip was applied. Generally, bottles made before 1858 have a "pontil" mark.[108] Many nineteenth-century bottles are embossed with information about the manufacturer. Maker's marks help archaeologists date bottles or provide information about their original contents.

LOOKING BACKWARD AND FORWARD

*O*ur challenge to investigate the history of the Underground Railroad in the Town of Chester led us to multiple sites and individuals, each with its own story. Collectively, they support a broader picture of active UGRR participation in this small Adirondack town. Some current residents were able to contribute by giving oral narratives and sharing vintage photographs, often telling what they heard from their parents and grandparents, for future generations to be able to say "my people did that."

Gathering supporting documents, town records, newspaper archives and scholarly historical research all contributed to a plethora of intricate details to organize. In the effort to make historical information accessible, the appendix gathers some of these original items. Further, the finding of antique quilts and other artifacts gave us insight into the discussion of material culture.

In addition to elucidating the dating and details of nineteenth-century quilts, the quilt experts were anxious to share their information on the proper handling of antique quilts. Never use plastic bags for storage. Wrap quilts in cotton sheets and refold them regularly.

We noted connections and duplications. Although our story began with the Darrowsville Wesleyan Methodist Church, the Presbyterian church in Chestertown was shown to be another place of gathering for abolitionists. The local Baptist church and the Quakers were believed to be involved as well.

From oral interviews, two separate narrators told us about hiding places using similar words to describe "sleeping shelves." Notably, the photographs of what remains of different hiding spaces appear strikingly similar. Different sites had duplicate artifacts; shoe forms, quilts, rope beds and clay pipes.

At least three and possibly four of the sites were taverns, or hostelries, operating along the military and stagecoach roads. In the 1840s, in the Town of Chester, the Liberty Party officials, the town supervisor, religious leaders and tavern keepers were all abolitionists, and many were active in the local UGRR.

There may be more to find through further discovery of historical material and archaeology.

The rewriting of the history of the Town of Chester needs to include this new chapter of the Underground Railroad story, enlarging the cultural and historical heritage, forging a new perspective of their prideful history and marking the path on the map that led fugitives due north to Canada.

APPENDIX A

Timeline

1619	First African slaves arrive in Jamestown, Virginia.
1775	First abolitionist society is organized by Ben Franklin in Philadelphia.
1783	Federal Fugitive Slave Law is passed, making it a crime to assist an escaped slave and permitting masters or slave catchers to seize runaways, even in free states.
1785	Manumission Society of New York is organized.
1791	Eli Whitney invents the cotton gin; cotton becomes "King."
1808	U.S. Congress prohibits importation of African Slaves; active smuggling and trading continue.
1820	Missouri Compromise is passed by U.S. Congress, an attempt to balance the number of free and slave states.

1827	Slavery is outlawed in New York State.
1831	William Lloyd Garrison publishes the *Liberator* newspaper.
1833	Slavery is abolished in British Empire, including Canada.
1833	Garrison and Arthur Lewis Tappan start the American Anti-Slavery Society.
1838	Frederick Douglass escapes with forged papers and disguises himself as a free black man.
1839	Liberty Party is founded in Warsaw, New York, as a national political party for abolitionism.
1843	Abel Brown meets Elizabeth and Joseph Leggett at Oliver Arnold's Temperance Tavern.
1845	Gerrit Smith conducts antislavery tour of Upstate New York.
1847	Frederick Douglass publishes the *North Star* newspaper.
1849	Henry "Box" Brown escapes slavery by shipping himself as cargo from Richmond, Virginia, to Philadelphia and the Underground Railroad.
1850	Fugitive Slave Law imposed a duty on all citizens to assist federal marshals to enforce the law and assist in the capture of fugitives or be prosecuted for their failure to do so.
1851	Harriet Tubman makes her first of several return trips to the South to guide family members and others north on the Underground Railroad.
1851	Christiana, Pennsylvania Riot, or Christiana Massacre takes place; white and black neighbors protect runaway slaves and kill slave master.
1853	Harriet Beecher Stowe publishes *Uncle Tom's Cabin*, describing the horrors of slavery; 300,000 copies are sold in one year.

1854	Kansas-Nebraska Act nullifies the Missouri Compromise; establishes Nebraska as a free state; slavery in Kansas to be determined by popular sovereignty of legal residents.
1855–56	"Bleeding Kansas," escalating violence between pro-slavery "Border Ruffians" and antislavery "Free Staters," is a prelude to the Civil War.
1857	Dred Scott decision by U.S. Supreme Court determines that slaves are not citizens and cannot bring suits in U.S. courts; slaves taken to free states remain property.
1859	John Brown raids Federal Armory at Harper's Ferry, West Virginia, to spark slave rebellions in the South; the failed raid precipitates the Civil War.
1861	Civil War breaks out with clash between Confederate and Union forces at Fort Sumter, South Carolina.
1863	Lincoln issues Emancipation Proclamation, freeing slaves in all rebel states.
1865	Civil War ends.
1865	Thirteenth Amendment of the U.S. Constitution is ratified, abolishing slavery in the United States.

APPENDIX B

Gerrit Smith's Tour—Warren County ❦

The following is an excerpt from Gerrit Smith's tour, published in the June 25, 1845 edition of the *Albany Patriot*. The tour started in Saratoga Springs on May 26, 1845. Reprinted with permission from the New-York Historical Society.

Gerrit Smith's Tour Through Saratoga, Warren, Essex and Clinton
Glen's Falls, May 28. Here too is the beginning and not a small beginning, of a city. The population is 2500—about 1000 less than that of Saratoga Springs. The rapids, at this place, in the Hudson River afford innumerable sites for mills. Here are lumber-mills, having each twenty or thirty saws; and here are mills for sawing marble, which contain hundreds of saws. Great quantities of the best lime are made here.

May 29. I am to speak in the Presbyterian church, this evening, on slavery. You will be surprised to hear me say, that I have never been in a village, which promises better than this for the anti-slavery cause. Doctor Davis is an intelligent and decided abolitionist; and I think, that I can say as much of Mr. Wilson. There are other leading men in the village, who will, I think, espouse the good cause, without delay. Among these are Mr. Paddock, Mr. Sherwood, and Mr. Burnham. What a happy thing it would be, if a few such men in the County of Warren should now resolve, that, God helping them, they will bring their County to declare itself, even at the very next Election, on the side of oppressed and crushed humanity! Such a resolution would surely be followed by such a result.

Caldwell, May 30. Water froze at Glen's Falls, last night. This evening I am to speak in the Presbyterian church on slavery. I do not wonder, that Caldwell is such a fashionable resort from June to September. It is one of the loveliest spots I have ever seen.

Warrensburg, May 31. The last was still colder than the previous night. As we came here this morning from Caldwell, we observed the marks of the severe frost upon the leaves. The gardens are well nigh spoiled: and it is the more general opinion, that the apples and plums are destroyed. Some persons, however, think otherwise.

June 1, Sabbath evening. I was permitted to address quite a large audience to-day in the Methodist church on the subject of slavery:—and this too, notwithstanding, that there is not one man in all this considerable village, who is called an abolitionist; and notwithstanding also, that the ministers here never speak of the slave in their sermons or public prayers. Mr. Bishop of this place sympathizes with the anti-slavery cause. But, whether he will have the courage to espouse it openly, and consent to be laughed at and hated by his neighbors, I do not know. Let him believe that God can support him, however violently the waves of public sentiment may beat against him.

The Schroon branch of the Hudson River passing here, makes this a place of business. Here are gentlemen of wealth and intelligence. How much happier, and how much more useful they would be, were they giving their influence to the cause of the enslaved!

Chester, June 2. I came, this morning, to this thriving village. I am to speak, this afternoon, in the Presbyterian church, on slavery.

June 3. I am much pleased with this people. They are candid and truth-loving. Their ministers are not ashamed, nor afraid, to plead the cause of the enslaved. Here are abolitionists of the truest class. I refer to such worthy men, as Mr. Leggett, Mr. Arnold, and Dr. Pritchard. Here too are Whigs and Democrats, whose intelligence and Christian integrity will not permit them to remain longer in their pro-slavery connection. Such are the merchants, Mr. Fowler, Mr. Smith, and Mr. Tubbs. If our friends at Glen's Falls should move, as I hope they may, for a revolution in this County, they may calculate, that Chester will do her full share in this blessed and glorious work. I am to proceed this afternoon to the County of Essex. In passing out of the County of Warren, I am happy in the thought, that she will be one of the first counties to take her stand on the side of impartial freedom. This will not be the case, however, unless the leading men of Glen's Falls shall do their duty. God grant that they may feel how great is their responsibility!

June 4. Head of Schroon Lake. I reached this little village, last evening. I am now in the County of Essex—a County, which, as well as Clinton, is destined to be one of the richest in the State. The soil in both Counties, especially in Essex, is generally inferior; but the iron ore in both are abundant in quantity; whilst in quality, they are probably superior to any others, which have been discovered in our nation. The farming population of these Counties will be much less than in many other equal portions of the State; but the next, if not the present generation, will witness dozens of new manufacturing villages in them. But, little iron ore, and that of an inferior quality, has been found in the County of Warren. That County, however, with its abundance of hemlock and land, that, for the most part, is very desirable, if not entirely unfit for agriculture, will, at no distant day, be probably the greatest leather-manufacturing County in the State.

APPENDIX C

Abel Brown's Memoirs—Chester

The following is an excerpt from *Memoir of Rev. Abel Brown,* by His Companion C.S. Brown, published by the author in 1849 (pages 175–78).

Chester, Warren Co., N.Y., Oct. 11, 1843.
Ever Dear Catherine:—I have to day been pent in by mountains as high as grass or trees can grow, rising above each other in indescribable masses of rugged piles, which make me tremble as I approach—any part of Massachusetts is a plain, when compared with what I have passed to day. One mountain, which I think is located in the town of Warrensburgh, about twice as high as Wachsett, (I cannot spell it) was perfectly bare—a mass of solid granite; enough to build ten, if not one hundred such cities as New York. I had so much Antislavery to attend to, that I had very little time to look up; and it is now of no use, as the rocks are so high, that I cannot see the top. Yet I am now in a very quiet place in a Temperance house, (parlor very neat and comfortable) thinking, what a fool I was, to let Catherine Swan Brown stay in that nest so good and lovely, and I wander off in this land of hills and glens alone.

I received your letter with more than a glad heart, but was so overwhelmed with duties, that I had no time to write.

I was in Albany only from Thursday 3 o'clock P.M. to Friday morning 6 o'clock, and did not get the morning's mail before I left. Went to the printing office, wrote letters for two County Meetings, &c. &c. Ordered a cab to drive me back to my office—took my valise, bag &c., and was driven at a mad rate to the Railroad, just in time to take the cars—went like an arrow to Schenectady; met my noble companion Lewis Washington, whom I found ready to join me in a hearty laugh. He took the cars at Troy on that beautiful road, and in one of the most splendid cars; and like any other gentlemen sat where he found a seat. The conductor came and ordered him behind the door. But Mr. W. asked if the seats behind the door were any cheaper, than any other seats; and was told, they were not. He then said, he was a gentleman, and should ride where he pleased; and they might help themselves if they could. After considerable wrath, they left him to glory in his conquest alone, once. After hearing this, I went to the office and asked the agent for the company, if they intended to insult a colored man, on the Troy road? And after considerable hesitation, was told, that they always required them to sit behind the door. So now for another warfare.

We went on to Ballston Springs—Took our breakfast a few minutes before eleven o'clock—had a great County convention, and next day went on to Corinth, in time for P.M. meeting, where we continued two days; and left, loaded with invitations to return and bring my dear wife with me. Next morning, (Monday) rode down in sight of a place where the waters of the Hudson river roll in majestic splendor, over a perpendicular rock of from sixty to eighty feet—a grand sight it would have been, for my dear Catherine and sister Clara. Then passed over a road, that made me glad to hope that I was never to see it again; unless I went to do penance—the rocks, the rocks! I cannot describe them. Five miles, brought us to the river again, and then a plain, and fine road to Glens Falls. Then to Sandy Hill, where I found my old friend Stephen Lee, an old Revolutionary soldier, with his wife most dear, and his daughter very kind. Good people—Heaven bless them.

Next morning proceeded on our way to Caldwell, passing over a fine road through a beautifully romantic country, amid mountains and winding ravines, crystal streams, and beautiful Lakes, until we arrived in sight of Lake George, which lies with evening stillness, between towering mountains, inviting you to enjoy its sweet breezes and gentle zephyrs, with its beautiful Islands and overhanging and rock bound shores. How lovely, refreshing and enervating, must be its placid bosom amid the heat of summer. But the inhabitants of the beautiful village on its banks, are a slavery and rum cursed race; and where I expected to have found a hearty welcome—I was met by cold repulses. The Post Master said, there was no meeting, and only one Abolitionist within five miles; and no steamboat to convey me from such a miserable place. However, after much inquiry, I found a man (who lived twenty miles from there) who told me that an Antislavery Convention was in session at a distance of five miles, in a Baptist meeting house. God bless the Baptists, said I, and hired a boy for fifty cents to carry us on. Being in a great hurry to get his money, he drove the horse in "hot haste," and soon I found myself surrounded by an audience, who with earnest gaze heard me until five o'clock. Then the ministers who were holding a protracted meeting, politely invited my friend to occupy the evening; and I will only say, that we gratified them until eleven o'clock. A friend then took me in a carriage and carried me two miles to Hon. Mr. Richards, who had sent and invited us to his hospitable dwelling.

I slept from twelve until six, and then found the parlor with a good fire, which was graced with the presence of a Whig Representative, a good man, who made us feel at home in company with his intelligent and truly worthy appearing wife and daughters. After our repast, Mr. Washington arrived, and we were taken by my friend Leggett, and brought to this place. Dined with him and his Quaker wife, and am now writing at this Temperance house, at five o'clock and twenty minutes. The tea bell is ringing, and I must go to the table—then go to meeting and tell of the slaves' wrongs.

APPENDIX D

Numbers of Runaway Slaves

How many slaves actually escaped to a new life in the North, in Canada, Florida or Mexico? No one knows for sure. Some scholars say that the soundest estimate is a range between 25,000 and 40,000, while others top that figure at 50,000. The National Underground Railroad Freedom Center in Cincinnati says that number could be as high as 100,000, according to Elizabeth Pierce, an official there, though that seems quite optimistic to me. (**Henry Louis Gates Jr.**)[109]

[New Jersey historian Giles Wright encouraged discussion of the number of fugitives involved.] Most UGRR participants came from Missouri, Kentucky, Maryland, Virginia (slave states closest to the North). Most fugitives headed in a northeast direction. The overall number of runaways was very small, a tiny fraction of the total slave population. (**Giles Wright**)[110]

It's difficult to determine exactly how many slaves escaped through the Underground Railroad. An estimated 100,000 escaped to freedom over the course of the 19th century. (**James A. Banks**)[111]

During the 1800s, it is estimated that more than 100,000 enslaved people sought freedom through the Underground Railroad. (**National Freedom Center**)[112]

Several hundred slaves escaped per year throughout the mid-1800s. (**James McPherson**)[113]

Between 1820 and 1860, "The most frequent calculation is that around one thousand per year actually escaped." (**National Park Service**)[114]

Article in the *Journal of Black Studies* estimates that between 1830 and 1860, only about 2,000 escaped using the Underground Railroad. (**Okur**)[115]

Estimated rate of slave escapes (1810–1860) show a total number of 135,000. (**J. Blaine Hudson**)[116]

The Underground Railroad…consisted of many individuals—many whites but predominantly blacks—who knew only of the local efforts to aid fugitives and not of the overall operation. Still, it effectively moved hundreds of slaves northward each year—according to one estimate, the South lost 100,000 slaves between 1810 and 1850. (**Africans in America Resource Bank**)[117]

Estimates—guesses really—suggest [fugitives numbered] somewhere between 1,000 and 5,000 per year between 1830 and 1860. (**Eric Foner**)[118]

NOTES

Introduction

1. The North Star was said to be "the escaping slaves' heavenly guidepost," serving as a symbol of the promise of freedom from slavery. See Brackman, *Facts and Fabrications*, 85.
2. Residents could subscribe to national or regional newspapers that would be delivered by the post office for free. Local agents solicited subscribers. From 1837, the *Glens Falls Spectator*, the *Gazette*, the *Glen's Falls Clarion* and the *Glens Falls Republican* successively provided local advertising, household hints, stagecoach timetables and no local news coverage.
3. http//urrfreepress.com/#Scale.

Chapter 1

4. Henry Louis Gates Jr., "How Many Africans Were Really Taken to the U.S. During the Slave Trade?" TheRoot.com. See David Eltis and David Richardson, Transatlantic Slave Trade Database.
5. Gene Dattel, http://www.pbs.org/wnet/african-americans-many-rivers-to-cross/history/why-was-cotton-king.
6. www.cotton.org/pubs/cottoncounts/story.
7. Henry Louis Gates Jr., "100 Amazing Facts About the Negro No. 16: A Second Forced Migration of Slaves Wasn't Transatlantic," TheRoot, http://www.theroot.com/articles/history/201301/2nd_middle_passage_slaves_werent_just_forced_across_the_atlantic.html.

8. *Born in Slavery: Slave Narratives from the Federal Writers' Project, 1936–1938* contains more than 2,300 first-person accounts of slavery. These narratives were collected in the 1930s as part of the Federal Writers' Project of the Works Progress Administration (WPA), https://memory. loc.gov/ammem/snhtml/snhome.html.

9. Henry Louis Gates Jr., "Who Really Ran the Underground Railroad?" March 25, 2013, TheRoot, http://www.theroot.com/articles/ history/2013/03/who_really_ran_the_underground_railroad.3.html.

10. Franklin and Schwerninger, *Runaway Slaves*, 27–28.

11. Ibid., 262.

12. Schama, *Rough Crossings*, 6–7.

13. http://www.historynet.com/underground-railroad.

14. http://www.pbs.org/black-culture/shows/list/underground-railroad/ stories-freedom/underground-railroad-terminology.

15. Foner, op. cit., 6.

16. Hodges, *David Ruggles*.

17. www.nps.gov/exploring-exploring-our-common-past.

18. Gates, *African Americans*.

19. William W. Freehling, *The Road to Disunion* (New York: Oxford University Press, 2007), 236.

20. http://thefreegeorge.com/thefreegeorge/upstate-new-york-and-the- underground-railroad.

21. McKivigan, "Antislavery Comeouter Sects," 142–60.

22. Papson and Calarco, *Secret Lives of the Underground Railroad*, 75.

23. Tobin, *From Midnight to Dawn*, 27.

24. Ripley, *The Black Abolitionist Papers*, Vol. III, 9.

25. Brackman, *Facts and Fabrications*, 85.

26. *Liberator*, January 2, 1837.

27. Brackman, *Facts and Fabrications*, 85.

28. http://www.history.ac.uk/1807commemorated/discussion/supplicant_ slave.html.

29. Abolition Seminar, "Women in Abolitionism," 2014, http://www. abolitionseminar.org/women-and-abolitionism.

30. Andrea Korgan, "Heroes in Petticoats: The Role of Women in the Underground Railroad," Southern Adventist University, 2006, Senior Research Projects, Paper 27, http://knowledge.e.southern.edu/senior_ research/27.

31. Ibid.

32. Brackman, *Facts and Fabrications*, 85.

33. The African-American Mosaic, Library of Congress, http://www.loc. gov/exhibits/african/afam002.html.

34. Switala, op. cit., 15.

35. Jennifer Schuessler, "A Journey to Enclaves of Slavery in the North," *New York Times*, August 14, 2015.

36. Bordewich, *Bound for Canaan*, 169.

37. Foner, op. cit., 48.

38. Foner op. cit., 218, January 5, 1860.

39. Foner op. cit., 59.

40. Beecher was the brother of Harriet Beecher Stowe, whose controversial best-selling novel *Uncle Tom's Cabin* was published in 1852.

41. Switala, *Underground Railroad in New Jersey*, 92.

42. Wellman, *Brooklyn's Promised Land*.

43. See Foner; also Papson and Calarco.

44. Papson and Calarco, *Secret Lives of the Underground Railroad*, 28.

45. Documentary video, North Country Underground Railroad Museum, Ausable Chasm, New York.

46. Johnson, *Liberty Party 1840–1848*, review by John T. Cumbler.

47. Switala, op. cit., 120, 105.

48. Wessels, *Adirondack Profiles*, 70–71.

49. Paul Stewart, Underground Railroad History Project of the Capital Region, Inc. (URHPCR).

50. Freehling, op. cit.

51. Freehling, op. cit.

52. Philip Foner, *African American Experience*, online resource.

53. Brown, *Memoir of Abel Brown*, 110.

54. *Albany Patriot*, "Gerrit Smith Anti-Slavery Tour," June 25, 1845.

Chapter 2

55. Brown, *History of Warren County*, 131–39.

56. Ibid.

57. Caroline Fish, "History of Chestertown Reviewed," *Warrensburg News*, March 6, 1941.

58. Brown, *History of Warren County*, 131–39.

59. John T. Hastings, "The Plank Roads of Warrensburgh, The Long and Short of It," *Warrensburgh Historical Society Quarterly* (Winter 2015).

Chapter 4

60. "The History of the Champlain Conference 1843–2000," found at www. northnet.org/wesleyanturnpike/distchrs2/disthist.ppt.
61. The Proceedings of the Board of Supervisors of Warren County for November 1855, 317 and 318.
62. Caroline Fish, "Darrowsville Wesleyan Church," Town of Chester Historian Archives, 1976.
63. Copy of invoice for the bell for Darrowsville Wesleyan Methodist Church, Town of Chester Historian archives.
64. *Minerva Historical Society Quarterly* (October 1982).
65. List of pastors of Darrowsville Wesleyan Methodist Church supplied by the Champlain Conference of the Wesleyan Methodist Church, March 15, 1962.
66. Dollarhide, *New York State Censuses and Substitutes.*
67. *Minerva Historical Society Quarterly* (October 1982).
68. Ibid.
69. "History of the Presbyterian Church at Chestertown, N.Y. 1906," Town of Chester Historian Archives.

Chapter 5

70. "The Background of the Chestertown Leggetts," Town of Chester Historian Archives.
71. From a talk given by Helen Leggett in 1964, Town of Chester Historian Archives.
72. "History of the Presbyterian Church at Chestertown, N.Y. 1906," Town of Chester Historian Archives.
73. Ethan Perry, *Glens Falls* (NY) *Times,* Warren County Sesquicentennial Edition 1963, section two, page 4.
74. David Starbuck, "Finding Pieces of a Proud Past of Chestertown's Bicentennial," *Adirondack Life* (July/August 2000).

Chapter 6

75. "History of the Presbyterian Church at Chestertown, N.Y. 1906," Town of Chester Historian Archives.

76. Jean Hadden, "Turning Back the Pages," *Adirondack Journal*, May 9, 2009.
77. Short biography of Dr. Morgan Pritchard written by Sandra Carpenter, Town of Chester Historian Archives.
78. *Warrensburgh* (NY) *News*, April 1, 1897, Myron Tripp obituary.
79. Smith, "History of Warren County, NY," 282–83.
80. *Ticonderoga* (NY) *Sentinel*, October 28, 1898, 3.
81. "The History of the Champlain Conference 1843–2000," www.northnet. org/wesleyanturnpike/distchrs2/disthist.ppt.

Chapter 7

82. Wessels, *Adirondack Profiles*.

Chapter 8

83. *Washington Post*, March 10, 2015, B1.
84. Appleby, Hunt and Jacob, *Telling the Truth about History*.
85. Stewart, URHPCR.
86. Brackman, *Facts and Fabrications*, 7.
87. Wulfert, Myths of Quilts.
88. Dreissen, Putting It in Perspective.
89. Fellner, "Betsy Ross Redux."
90. Brackman, *Clues in the Calico*, 182–83.
91. Brackman, *Encyclopedia of Pieced Quilt Patterns*.
92. Meller and Elffers, *Textile Designs*, 276–77.
93. Trestain, *Dating Fabrics*.
94. Stewart, URHPCR.
95. http://www.countrybed.com/ancillary_pages/reference/bed_history. shtml. A straining wrench is the wooden tool Mr. S found.
96. http://www.colonialsense.com/How-To_Guides/Interior/Bed_ Roping.php.
97. http://www.davidwebbfowler.com/2014/05/some-things-about-colonial-beds.html.

Chapter 9

98. Singleton, *The Archaeology of Slavery and Plantation Life*.

99. Mike Toner, www.ushistory.org.

100. Gary Nash, www.ushistory.org.

101. Historic Camden County website, http://historiccamdencounty.com/ccnews11.shtml, New Jersey's Underground Railroad Mythbuster, June 2001; Hansen and McGowan, *Freedom Roads*. Archaeology meets oral tradition.

102. Broderick, Bouck, Huey and Feister, *Pottery Works*.

103. Warren Hartmann, www.earlyamericanstoneware.com.

104. http://ceramicartsdaily.org.

105. Deetz, *In Small Things Forgotten*.

106. J. Speight, http://www.historiccamdencounty.com/ccnews32.shtml.

107. https://www.antiquebottles-glass.com/learn/determining-the-age-of-antique-bottles.

108. www.bottlebooks.com.

Appendix D

109. Henry Louis Gates Jr., http://afroamhistory.about.com/od/slavery/a/How-Did-Slaves-Resist-Slavery.htm.

110. Giles Wright, http://historiccamdencounty.com/ccnews11.shtml.

111. Banks, *March Toward Freedom*.

112. National Underground Railroad Freedom Center, http://www.freedomcenter.org.

113. McPherson, *Battle Cry of Freedom*.

114. National Park Service, https://www.nps.gov/index.htm.

115. *Journal of Black Studies*, http://www.academia.edu/9565738/Underground_Railroad_in_Philadelphia_1830-1860.

116. Hudson, *Encyclopedia of the Underground Railroad*, 9.

117. Africans in America Resource Bank, http://www.pbs.org/wgbh/aia/part4/4p2944.html.

118. Foner, *Gateway to Freedom*, 4.

BIBLIOGRAPHY

Appleby, Joyce, Lynn Hunt and Margaret Jacob. *Telling the Truth about History.* New York: Norton Paperback, 1995.

Banks, James. *March Toward Freedom: A History of Black Americans.* N.p., 1970.

Bial, Raymond. *The Underground Railroad.* Boston: Houghton Mifflin Company, 1995.

Bordewich, Fergus M. *Bound for Canaan: The Epic Story of the Underground Railroad, America's First Civil Rights Movement.* New York: Amistad/Harper Collins, 2005.

Brackman, Barbara. *America's Printed Fabrics: 1770–1890.* Lafayette, CA: C&T Publishing, 2004.

———. *Civil War Quilts* blog. http://civilwarquilts.blogspot.com.

———. *Clues in the Calico: A Guide to Identifying and Dating Antique Quilts.* McClean, VA: EPM Publications, 1989.

———. *Encyclopedia of Pieced Quilt Patterns.* Paducah, KY: American Quilter's Society, 1993.

———. *Facts and Fabrications: Unraveling the History of Quilts and Slavery.* Lafayette, CA: C&T Publishing Company, 2006.

Broderick, Warren, William Bouck, Paul R. Huey and Lois M. Feister. *Pottery Works: Potteries of NY State's Capital District and Upper Hudson Region.* Canbury, NJ: Dickinson University Press, 1995.

Brown, C.S. *Memoir of Abel Brown.* Worcester, MA, 1849.

Brown, W.H. *History of Warren County, New York.* Glens Falls, NY, 1963.

Calarco, Tom. *The Underground Railroad in the Adirondack Region.* Jefferson, NC: McFarland & Company, 2004.

Deetz, James. *In Small Things Forgotten: An Archaeology of Early American Life.* New York: Knopf Doubleday Publishing Group, 2010. http://www.nps.gov/archeology/afori/howfig_mar4.htm.

Dollarhide, William. *New York State Censuses and Substitutes.* N.p.: Genealogical Publishing Company, 2005.

Dreissen, Kris. "Putting It in Perspective: The Symbolism of Underground Railroad Quilts." http://www.quilthistory.com/ugrrquilts.htm

Fellner, Leigh. "Betsy Ross Redux: The Underground 'Quilt Code.'" http://ugrrquilt.hartcottagequilts.com.

———. "Quilt Code FAQs." Handout sheet for free distribution. http://ugrrquilt.hartcottagequilts.com/QuiltCodeFAQs.pdf

Filler, Louis. *The Crusade Against Slavery: 1830–1860.* New York: Harper & Brothers, 1960.

Foner, Eric. *Gateway to Freedom: The Hidden History of the Underground Railroad.* New York: W.W. Norton Company, 2015.

Fradin, Dennis B. *Bound for the North Star: True Stories of Fugitive Slaves.* New York: Clarion Books, 2000.

Franklin, John Hope, and Loren Schwerninger. *Runaway Slaves: Rebels on the Plantation.* New York: Oxford University Press, 1999.

Freehling, William W. *The Road to Disunion: Secessionists Triumphant, 1854–1861.* Vol. 2, Oxford, UK: Oxford University Press, 2007.

Gara, Larry. *The Liberty Line: The Legend of the Underground Railroad.* Lexington: University Press of Kentucky, 1961.

Gates, Henry Louis, Jr. *African Americans: Many Rivers to Cross.* Episode 2. PBS documentary.

Godine, Amy. "Come and Join Us Brothers." *Adirondack Life* (December 2015).

Hansen, Joyce, and Gary McGowan. *Freedom Roads: Searching for the Underground Railroad.* Chicago: Cricket Books, 2003.

Hastings, John T. *Around Warrensburg.* Charleston, SC: Arcadia Publishing, 2009.

Hodges, Graham Russell Gao. *David Ruggles: A Radical Black Abolitionist and the Underground Railroad in New York City.* John Hope Franklin Series in African American History and Culture. N.p., n.d.

Horwitz, Tony. *Midnight Rising: John Brown and the Raid that Started the Civil War.* New York: Henry Holt Company, 2011.

Hudson, J. Blaine. *Encyclopedia of the Underground Railroad.* Jefferson, NC: McFarland & Company, 2006.

Johnson, Reinhard O. *The Liberty Party 1840–1848: Antislavery Third Party Politics in the United States.* Baton Rouge: Louisiana State University Press, 2009.

Ketchum, William C., Jr. *Potters and Potteries of New York State, 1650–1900.* New York: Funk and Wagnalls, 1970.

McKivigan, John R. "The Antislavery 'Comeouter' Sects: A Neglected Dimension of the Abolitionist Movement." *Civil War History* 26, no. 2 (June 1980): 142–60.

McPherson, James M. *Battle Cry of Freedom.* New York: Oxford University Press, 1988.

———. "The Fugitives Who Changed America." Review of *Gateway to Freedom* by Eric Foner. *New York Review of Books,* June 4, 2015.

Meller, Susan, and Joost Elffers. *Textile Designs: Two Hundred Years of European and American Patterns Organized by Motif, Style, Color, Layout, and Period.* New York: Harry H. Abrams, Incorporated, 2002.

Papson, Don, and Tom Calarco. *Secret Lives of the Underground Railroad in New York City: Sydney Howard Grey, Louis Napoleon and the Record of Fugitives.* Jefferson, NC: McFarland & Company, 2015.

Reynolds, David S. *John Brown Abolitionist: The Man Who Killed Slavery, Sparked the Civil War and Seeded Civil Rights.* New York: Alfred A. Knopf, 2005.

———. "The Hidden Story of the Underground Railroad: New York's Abolitionist Operatives Showed Cunning and Courage as They Worked to Help Fugitive Slaves." *Wall Street Journal,* January 16, 2015.

Ripley, Peter C. *The Black Abolitionist Papers.* Vol. III: *The United States, 1830–1846.* Chapel Hill: University of North Carolina Press, 1991.

Rossi, Ann. *Freedom Struggle: The Anti-Slavery Movement in America 1830–1865.* Washington, D.C.: National Geographic, 2005.

Schama, Simon. *Rough Crossings: Britain, the Slaves and the American Revolution.* New York: HarperCollins Publishers, 2006.

Schuessler, Jennifer. "A Journey to Enclaves of Slavery in the North." *New York Times,* August 14, 2015.

Seldon, Horace. The *Liberator* files. http://www.theliberatorfiles.com.

Siebert, Wilbur H. *The Underground Railroad from Slavery to Freedom.* New York: Russell and Russell, 1898 (reprint 1967).

Singleton, Theresa. *The Archaeology of Slavery and Plantation Life.* New York: Routledge, reprint edition, September 1985.

Smith, H.P., ed. "History of Warren County, NY." 1885.

Still, William. *The Underground Railroad.* N.p., 1872 (reprint, Project Gutenberg ebook, 1972).

Switala, William. *Underground Railroad in New Jersey and New York.* Mechanicsburg, PA: Stackpole Books, 2006.

Tobin, Jacqueline L. *From Midnight to Dawn: The Last Tracks of the Underground Railroad.* New York: Anchor Books, 2008.

Trestain, Eileen Jahnke. *Dating Fabrics: A Color Guide 1800–1960.* Paducah, KY: American Quilter Society, 1998.

Wellman, Judith. *Brooklyn's Promised Land: The Free Black Community of Weeksville, NY.* New York: NYU Press, 2014.

Wessels, William. *Adirondack Profiles.* Blue Mountain Lake, NY: Hamilton Advertising Agency, 1961.

Wulfert, Jennifer. "The Myths of Quilts on the Underground Railroad." http://www.antiquequiltdating.com/UGRR_index.html.

Zinn, Howard. *A People's History of the United States.* New York: Harper Perennial, 2003.

INDEX

ABOUT THE AUTHORS

*M*s. Lagoy has a BA from SUNY-Plattsburgh and has a postgraduate teacher certification. She taught elementary school for the North Warren Central School system for thirty-three years. In 2006 Ms. Lagoy was appointed Chief Historian of the Town of Chester. She has been on the board of trustees of the Historical Society since 1990 and has been editor of the quarterly newsletter since 2007.

Ms. Lagoy has contributed material for *Adirondack 102* by Martin Podskoch (2014) and *Around Warrensburgh* by John T. Hastings (2014). She wrote the Town of Chester section for the *Warren County Bicentennial Celebration Guide* (2013). She cowrote *The Darrowsville Church on the UGRR* (2013).

*M*s. Seldman has a BS from Cornell University, an MFA from George Washington University and was president of Community Educational Exhibitions and Community Educational Silkscreen Center from 1975 to 2013. She is a photographer, master serigrapher, gallery manager and workshop director.

Ms. Seldman, the author of *The People's Silkscreen Book* (1975), *Artist Portrait Archives* (2008) and *The Darrowsville Church on the UGRR* (2013), has participated in more than one hundred fine art exhibitions. She was appointed Photo Historian of the Historical Society of the Town of Chester in 2014. She was a master serigrapher, workshop director, gallery manager and photographer.

Ms. Seldman's family were guests at Carisbrooke and the White Lodge (the safe house site in Schroon Lake) during the summers of 1950 and 1951.

CPSIA information can be obtained
at www.ICGtesting.com
Printed in the USA
BVHW06*0432091018
529575BV00003B/66/P